The Stress-Free Holiday Wellness Guide: Mindful Self-Care and Intentional Living Tips for a Calm, Joyful Season

Practical Tips and Guided Reflections for Reducing Holiday Stress, Cultivating Gratitude, and Embracing Balance Year-Round

Emma Grace Williams

Copyright © 2024 by Emma Grace Williams

All rights reserved.

No part of this book may be reproduced in any form or by any electronic or mechanical means, including information storage and retrieval systems, without written permission from the author, except for the use of brief quotations in a book review.

Contents

Embracing Wellness During the Holidays	v
1. UNDERSTANDING THE HOLIDAY STRESSORS	1
Common Holiday Stressors	3
Recognizing Signs of Holiday Burnout	6
2. RECLAIMING THE HOLIDAYS: SETTING BOUNDARIES AND PRIORITIZING YOUR MENTAL HEALTH	9
Healthy Boundaries with Family and Friends	11
Avoiding Comparison and Perfectionism	14
3. CULTIVATING MINDFULNESS AND PRESENT MOMENT AWARENESS	19
Integrating Mindfulness into Holiday Traditions	21
Creating Moments of Pause	24
4. SELF-CARE RITUALS FOR THE HOLIDAY SEASON	29
Daily Self-Care Practices	31
Self-Compassion Over Perfection	34
5. NUTRITION AND PHYSICAL WELLNESS DURING THE HOLIDAYS	39
Balanced Nutrition and Mindful Indulgence	40
Incorporating Gentle Movement	42
6. SOCIAL CONNECTIONS: FOSTERING HEALTHY RELATIONSHIPS	46
Creating Meaningful Interactions	47
Navigating Family Dynamics	50

7. HANDLING GRIEF AND LONELINESS DURING
   THE HOLIDAYS ... 55
   Acknowledge and Honor Loss ... 56
   Finding Comfort in Solitude ... 59

8. UNPLUGGING AND RECHARGING: DIGITAL
   DETOX FOR THE HOLIDAYS ... 64
   Limiting Screen Time ... 65
   Creating Tech-Free Holiday Traditions ... 68

9. CREATING NEW, WELLNESS-ORIENTED
   HOLIDAY TRADITIONS ... 74
   Reimagining Old Traditions ... 75
   Incorporating Acts of Kindness and Giving ... 78

10. REFLECTING AND PREPARING FOR THE NEW
    YEAR WITH A WELLNESS FOCUS ... 83
    The Power of Reflection ... 84
    Creating a Wellness-Oriented New Year's Ritual ... 87

Afterword ... 93
Appendices: Wellness Recourses ... 103
More About Emma Grace Williams ... 119

Embracing Wellness During the Holidays

As the holiday season approaches, many eagerly anticipate a time of joy, celebration, and cherished traditions. For most, this season represents an opportunity to reconnect with loved ones, create lasting memories, and find solace in shared rituals. However, the holidays can also usher in a unique set of challenges—elevated stress levels, heightened expectations, and emotional complexities that can take a toll on one's mental, emotional, and physical health. In recent years, there's been a growing awareness of these challenges, leading to an increased focus on wellness and self-care during the holiday season. This shift is rooted in a collective recognition of the need to balance celebration with mindfulness, and to ensure that the joy of the season doesn't come at the expense of our well-being.

More than ever, people are choosing to embrace wellness as an integral part of their holiday experience. The traditional hustle and bustle of the season, while exciting, often leaves little room for self-care, reflection, or genuine relaxation. This guide is designed to support readers in bringing wellness into their holiday traditions, fostering a sense of balance, fulfillment, and mental clarity during this busy season. By focusing on mindfulness, personal development, and mental health, this guide aims to transform the holiday season into an opportunity for both celebration and growth, allowing readers to enter the new year feeling revitalized, centered, and ready for new challenges.

The Importance of Wellness During the Holidays

The holiday season is a paradox of joy and stress, connection and complexity. The warmth of togetherness is sometimes paired with the strain of expectations, and the excitement of celebration often coexists with the fatigue of endless commitments. For many, the holiday period can trigger a range of emotions—happiness mixed with nostalgia, anticipation laced with anxiety, and joy accompanied by a lingering sense of pressure. Understanding these dynamics is essential in approaching the season with mindfulness, recognizing that while celebrations are important, they should not overshadow the need for personal well-being.

Understanding the Unique Mental Health Challenges of the Season

Embracing Wellness During the Holidays

Holidays can intensify mental health challenges in several ways. Financial pressures, family dynamics, social obligations, and even the pervasive culture of comparison on social media can amplify feelings of inadequacy, stress, and even loneliness. For some, the holiday season may bring unresolved emotional wounds to the surface, especially in the context of family gatherings or holiday traditions that stir memories. Furthermore, the pressure to meet various expectations—from hosting gatherings to purchasing gifts—can place an enormous strain on one's mental health, often resulting in exhaustion and burnout.

The holidays also coincide with shorter days, less sunlight, and colder weather, which can contribute to Seasonal Affective Disorder (SAD) and further impact mood and energy levels. These factors combined underscore the need for a conscious approach to mental health during this season, encouraging individuals to prioritize their emotional needs and practice self-compassion. Wellness during the holidays, therefore, becomes more than a luxury—it's a necessary foundation for managing the emotional complexities of the season and entering the new year with a healthy mindset.

Balancing Celebration and Stress

Finding balance during the holidays is an art that requires intentionality, mindfulness, and self-awareness. While it's natural to desire a season filled with joy and excitement, the reality is that achieving balance requires us to set realistic expectations and prioritize our own needs. This means recognizing when it's okay to say no to social invitations, to scale back on gift-giving, or to create new traditions that feel more authentic and less stressful.

Balance also means being attuned to our own mental and emotional thresholds, knowing when to step back, recharge, and seek moments of peace amid the whirlwind of activity. The practice of balance allows us to honor both our need for connection and our need for solitude, for celebration and for rest. By approaching the holiday season with mindfulness and self-care, we give ourselves the permission to engage fully in the moments that matter while safeguarding our well-being.

Defining Wellness in the Context of Holidays

In recent years, wellness has come to encompass a holistic approach to health that includes mental, emotional, and physical dimensions. Wellness during the holiday season, therefore, is not limited to physical health; it extends to the way we care for our minds, process our emotions, and maintain our personal boundaries. True wellness during the holidays embraces mental clarity, emotional balance, and physical vitality, creating a foundation that supports us through the season's ups and downs.

1. **Mental Wellness**: Mental wellness during the holidays involves maintaining a calm and clear mind amid the excitement and demands of the season. It's about nurturing our mental health through practices that reduce stress, enhance focus, and allow us to be present. This may include practices like meditation, journaling, setting realistic goals, or practicing gratitude—activities that ground us in the present moment and allow us to navigate holiday challenges with resilience.
2. **Emotional Wellness**: Embracing emotional wellness means being mindful of our feelings and creating space for self-compassion. The holiday season can bring forth a wide range of emotions, from joy to nostalgia, and even sorrow. Emotional wellness encourages us to process these feelings, seek support

when needed, and avoid bottling up emotions that might lead to holiday burnout. Setting boundaries, recognizing triggers, and engaging in meaningful connections can enhance emotional resilience, allowing us to experience the holidays with a sense of fulfillment and balance.

3. **Physical Wellness**: Physical wellness is often overlooked during the holidays, but it plays a critical role in our overall well-being. Physical self-care during the season might involve prioritizing restful sleep, maintaining a balanced diet, or setting aside time for regular exercise. While indulging in holiday treats and traditions is a cherished part of the season, physical wellness encourages us to find a balance that supports our energy levels, immune health, and physical vitality.

Incorporating Wellness into Holiday Traditions

Traditional holiday activities—from decorating and cooking to gathering with friends and family—can become mindful practices when we approach them with intention. Simple adjustments to holiday routines can transform even the busiest days into opportunities for reflection, self-care, and personal growth. Incorporating wellness into holiday traditions might involve creating new rituals, such as a morning gratitude practice, a family meditation session, or a weekly nature walk to counterbalance the busyness of the season.

In addition to personal wellness practices, creating a holiday environment that fosters well-being for everyone involved is equally valuable. This may include hosting gatherings that emphasize meaningful connection over materialism, simplifying gift-giving practices, or encouraging loved ones to engage in shared mindfulness activities. By incorporating wellness into holiday traditions, we create a season that prioritizes quality over quantity, fostering a holiday experience that's rooted in mindfulness and fulfillment.

A Season of Reflection and Renewal

The holiday season holds a unique significance as it bridges the closing of one year with the dawning of another. This transitional period presents an opportunity to reflect on the past year, celebrate personal growth, and set intentions for the year ahead. By approaching the holidays as a time for both celebration and renewal, we can cultivate a season that not only brings joy in the present but also strengthens our mental, emotional, and physical well-being for the future.

In this guide, we will explore practical ways to integrate wellness into your holiday experience, offering insights into mental health strategies, mindfulness practices, and self-care rituals that support a balanced, mindful approach to the season. Whether you're seeking to manage holiday stress, deepen your personal growth, or create a holiday season that aligns with your values, this guide provides a roadmap for a fulfilling, wellness-centered holiday that honors both celebration and self-care. As we journey through this guide, remember that true wellness is about finding joy in the moment, connecting with yourself and others meaningfully, and entering the new year with a renewed sense of purpose and well-being.

Chapter 1
Understanding the Holiday Stressors

The holiday season is often envisioned as a time of warmth, connection, and shared joy. Festive gatherings, gift exchanges, and cherished traditions create a sense of magic, anticipation, and comfort. However, beneath this joyful façade lies a complex tapestry of stressors that can turn the holidays into a challenging time for many. From financial pressures to social obligations and societal expectations, the holiday season can heighten anxiety, strain relationships, and leave us feeling emotionally depleted. In this chapter, we'll explore the root causes of holiday stress, examining common stressors and understanding how they affect mental health. By recognizing the unique stressors that accompany the holidays, we can begin to approach this season with awareness, intention, and a deeper commitment to self-care.

Common Holiday Stressors

Financial Pressures

One of the most pervasive sources of holiday stress is the financial burden that comes with the season. Gift-giving, holiday travel, elaborate meals, decorations, and social gatherings can quickly add up, leading to anxiety about budgeting and spending. Many people feel pressured to spend beyond their means to show appreciation or maintain holiday traditions, often at the expense of their financial well-being. Advertisements, sales events, and the omnipresent culture of consumerism amplify these pressures, creating an expectation that love, gratitude, and generosity must be equated with material giving.

Beyond direct spending, there's an added layer of financial strain for those supporting extended families, managing blended families, or navigating complex family dynamics. The desire to provide memorable experiences for loved ones can create unrealistic expectations around holiday spending, leaving many with a sense of inadequacy if they cannot meet these demands. The post-holiday financial aftermath is often equally stressful, with many facing the consequences of overspending well into the new year.

Social Obligations and the Pressure to Connect

The holidays are known for social gatherings, parties, and family get-togethers, which can be both a source of joy and a profound stressor. The expectation to participate in multiple events, often within a short time frame, can lead to social burnout. Individuals may feel compelled to attend gatherings out of obligation, fearing the potential disappointment or judgment of others if they decline. For those with social anxiety, these events can feel overwhelming, creating feelings of discomfort, self-doubt, and even dread.

For some, the holidays bring a sense of loneliness rather than connection. Those who are far from family, who have strained relationships, or who have experienced loss may find the season intensifies feelings of isolation. Social media amplifies this sense of disconnection, presenting curated images of joyful gatherings that can create a distorted sense of reality and heighten feelings of inadequacy. This expectation to be socially "on" and constantly connected can take a toll, leading to emotional exhaustion and making it difficult to find time for personal reflection and rest.

Family Dynamics and Unresolved Tensions

Family gatherings are a hallmark of the holiday season, yet they are also one of its most complex stressors. For many, family reunions bring up unresolved tensions, past conflicts, or strained relationships that resurface during the holidays. Differences in values, lifestyles, or opinions can lead to conflict, causing individuals to feel misunderstood or alienated within their own family dynamics. In some cases, individuals may feel obligated to conform to family expectations or traditions that do not align with their current values or beliefs, leading to feelings of discomfort or resentment.

The desire to create a "perfect" family gathering can add further stress, especially for those who feel responsible for hosting or organizing. From preparing meals to managing guests' expectations, the burden of ensuring that family gatherings go smoothly can lead to burnout. For individuals who have experienced loss or who may be navigating blended or non-traditional family structures, these gatherings can evoke complicated emotions, making it difficult to fully enjoy the holiday experience.

Societal Expectations and the "Ideal" Holiday

Society presents a vision of the "perfect holiday" that is deeply embedded in media, advertising, and cultural narratives. This idealized version of the holidays—filled with perfect decorations, joyful gatherings, harmonious family interactions, and endless gifts—creates a standard that is often unrealistic and unachievable. The pressure to meet this ideal can create feelings of inadequacy and disappointment when the reality of the season does not align with these expectations.

For many, this pressure is compounded by a sense of comparison fueled by social media, where carefully curated images of holiday joy and success are on display. The result is a pervasive sense of "not enough": not enough time, not enough money, not enough joy. These societal expectations amplify feelings of anxiety and depression, leading many to feel that they are failing at the holiday experience. By acknowledging these stressors and challenging the notion of a "perfect holiday," we can begin to reframe our approach to the season in a way that prioritizes well-being over external expectations.

Recognizing Signs of Holiday Burnout

While the holiday season can bring joy and excitement, it can also lead to burnout—a state of emotional, mental, and physical exhaustion. Holiday burnout occurs when individuals become overwhelmed by the demands, expectations, and complexities of the season, resulting in a loss of energy, enthusiasm, and even health. Recognizing the signs of burnout is crucial to taking proactive steps to protect our well-being and finding a sense of balance and fulfillment during the holidays.

Identifying Triggers and Emotional Exhaustion

Burnout often stems from the accumulation of small, repetitive stressors that build up over time. These triggers can vary from person to person, but common contributors include overcommitting to social events, feeling obligated to meet others' expectations, and neglecting personal needs. The emotional exhaustion associated with burnout can lead to feelings of irritability, frustration, and resentment, making it difficult to enjoy the holiday experience. Physically, burnout can manifest as fatigue, headaches, and other stress-related symptoms, while mentally, it can create a sense of overwhelm, difficulty focusing, and even feelings of apathy.

Emotional exhaustion can be further exacerbated by specific holiday stressors, such as family dynamics or financial pressures. For example, individuals who feel financially stretched may experience heightened anxiety, while those navigating challenging family relationships may feel emotionally drained. Recognizing these triggers is the first step in addressing burnout, as it allows us to identify the sources of our stress and take proactive measures to manage them.

. . .

Setting Realistic Expectations for the Season

One of the most effective ways to combat holiday burnout is to set realistic expectations for ourselves and others. This means acknowledging that we cannot do everything, and that it's okay to let go of certain obligations, traditions, or expectations that don't serve our well-being. By setting boundaries and prioritizing what truly matters, we can create a holiday experience that feels fulfilling and manageable.

Setting realistic expectations also involves being honest with ourselves about our energy levels, mental health, and personal capacity. It's important to communicate openly with family, friends, and loved ones about our needs and limitations. This may mean declining certain invitations, reducing the scale of holiday celebrations, or seeking support when needed. The goal is to create a holiday season that feels authentic, balanced, and meaningful, rather than one that is defined by external pressures or societal ideals.

Recognizing When to Step Back and Recharge

Burnout is often a signal that we need to take a step back, slow down, and prioritize self-care. During the holiday season, it can be easy to fall into the trap of constant activity, but finding time to recharge is essential for mental, emotional, and physical well-being. This might involve setting aside time each day for quiet reflection, practicing mindfulness, engaging in activities that bring joy, or simply allowing ourselves to rest.

For some, stepping back may mean reevaluating holiday traditions and exploring new ways to celebrate that feel less demanding and more aligned with personal values. By giving ourselves permission to let go of certain expectations and embrace a simpler, more intentional approach, we can create a holiday experience that is both restorative and joyful.

Understanding the root causes of holiday stress and recognizing the signs of burnout are essential steps toward navigating the season with resilience and self-awareness. By identifying common stressors—such as financial pressures, social obligations, family dynamics, and societal expectations—we can gain insight into the unique challenges of the holiday season and take proactive measures to protect our well-being. Recognizing the symptoms of burnout and setting realistic expectations allows us to approach the holidays with a sense of balance, creating space for joy, rest, and reflection.

In the following chapters, we will delve deeper into practical strategies for managing holiday stress, exploring ways to incorporate mindfulness, self-care, and wellness practices into the season. By prioritizing mental health and emotional well-being, we can create a holiday experience that is both fulfilling and sustainable, allowing us to enjoy the present moment while setting the foundation for a meaningful and balanced year ahead.

Chapter 2
Reclaiming the Holidays: Setting Boundaries and Prioritizing Your Mental Health

The holiday season often comes with an unspoken set of expectations—attend every gathering, participate in every tradition, give the perfect gifts, and present a flawless image to the world. Yet, maintaining this level of engagement and perfection can leave us feeling drained, anxious, and disconnected from the true joy of the season. In reclaiming the holidays, the goal isn't to reject traditions or connections but rather to reshape our experience in a way that protects our mental health and honors our personal needs. This chapter focuses on setting healthy boundaries with family and friends and letting go of perfectionism to create a more balanced, authentic holiday season.

Healthy Boundaries with Family and Friends

Setting boundaries during the holidays may feel counterintuitive. We're often conditioned to believe that the season should be a time of giving, gathering, and saying "yes" to every opportunity. However, without boundaries, we can quickly find ourselves overwhelmed, stressed, and emotionally drained. Healthy boundaries allow us to engage in holiday traditions and connections meaningfully while protecting our mental and emotional well-being. This section explores the importance of boundaries during the holidays, offering strategies for setting limits on time, energy, and social commitments and learning how to say "no" gracefully to create a balanced, fulfilling holiday experience.

Understanding the Role of Boundaries in Holiday Well-being

Boundaries serve as a way to protect our mental, emotional, and physical energy. They act as a guide, helping us to prioritize our needs, manage stress, and prevent burnout. During the holidays, boundaries become even more critical, as we're often pulled in multiple directions, with demands on our time and energy from family, friends, and social obligations. Without boundaries, it's easy to overextend ourselves, leading to feelings of resentment, fatigue, and emotional exhaustion.

Establishing boundaries doesn't mean withdrawing from holiday activities or disconnecting from loved ones. Rather, it means approaching the season with intentionality, allowing us to participate in ways that feel meaningful and manageable. By setting clear limits, we can enjoy the holiday season without sacrificing our well-being, creating space for genuine connection and joy.

. . .

Strategies for Setting Limits on Time, Energy, and Social Commitments

Setting boundaries with family and friends requires self-awareness, communication, and a willingness to prioritize our needs. Here are some practical strategies to help you navigate social obligations and manage your time and energy during the holidays:

1. **Assess Your Capacity**: Begin by reflecting on your personal energy levels, commitments, and capacity for social interaction. Identify the activities and gatherings that feel most meaningful and prioritize those. Recognize that it's okay not to attend every event and that limiting your commitments doesn't make you any less dedicated to the holiday spirit.
2. **Communicate Openly**: Boundaries are most effective when they're communicated clearly. Be open with family and friends about your availability, energy levels, and any specific needs. For example, you might let loved ones know that you'll only attend certain gatherings or that you'll need to leave by a specific time. Clear communication helps others understand your boundaries and reduces the likelihood of misunderstandings.
3. **Limit Social Interactions**: If you find that constant social interaction drains your energy, consider limiting the number of gatherings you attend. Choosing quality over quantity allows you to engage fully in the events you do attend, making them more enjoyable and less exhausting.
4. **Schedule Time for Rest**: Protecting your energy during the holidays means balancing social time with moments of rest and solitude. Schedule downtime for

yourself, whether it's an evening in, a quiet morning walk, or a weekend dedicated to relaxation. Rest is an essential component of well-being, allowing you to recharge and approach each holiday event with a refreshed mindset.

5. **Practice Selective Participation**: Remember that you don't have to engage in every holiday activity to experience the season fully. Selective participation allows you to choose the traditions and gatherings that resonate most with you, without feeling obligated to participate in every holiday ritual. This approach can make the season feel more personal, authentic, and less overwhelming.

How to Say "No" Gracefully to Protect Your Mental Health

Saying "no" can be one of the most challenging aspects of setting boundaries, especially during the holidays. We often worry that declining invitations or opting out of activities will disappoint others or create conflict. However, saying "no" is an essential skill for protecting your mental health and ensuring that your holiday experience remains manageable and fulfilling.

Here are some tips for saying "no" gracefully:

- **Express Appreciation First**: Begin by acknowledging the invitation or request with gratitude. For example, "Thank you so much for inviting me; it means a lot to me." This approach shows that you appreciate the thought behind the invitation, even if you're unable to attend.
- **Be Direct and Kind**: Avoid giving ambiguous responses that might leave room for negotiation. Politely but firmly explain your decision. For example,

"I won't be able to make it this year, but I'd love to catch up soon." Directness conveys clarity, while kindness ensures that your response is received positively.
- **Offer an Alternative**: If possible, suggest an alternative that aligns with your boundaries. For instance, if you're unable to attend a large gathering, you might suggest meeting up for coffee at a later date. Offering an alternative shows that you value the connection while maintaining your personal needs.
- **Avoid Over-Explaining**: You don't need to justify your decision or provide detailed explanations. A simple, honest response is often sufficient. Over-explaining can sometimes create unnecessary pressure or guilt, detracting from the strength of your boundary.

Setting boundaries and saying "no" gracefully are acts of self-care that allow you to reclaim control over your holiday experience. By honoring your needs and limitations, you can engage in the season more fully and authentically, creating a holiday experience that feels both manageable and meaningful.

Avoiding Comparison and Perfectionism

In today's digital age, the holidays are accompanied by a constant stream of images, videos, and updates showcasing picture-perfect celebrations, lavish gifts, and beautifully decorated spaces. Social media amplifies the pressures of the season, creating an idealized image of the holidays that can make even the most joyful moments feel inadequate by comparison. For many, this pressure to present a flawless holiday experience leads to perfectionism, creating unrealistic expectations that can overshadow the true joy of the season. This section explores the impact of comparison and perfectionism during the holidays, offering strategies to embrace imperfection, manage social media pressures, and cultivate a holiday experience that feels genuine and fulfilling.

Embracing Imperfection in Holiday Traditions

The pursuit of perfection can be exhausting, often leaving us feeling like we're constantly falling short. The holidays are not meant to be a performance; they're an opportunity to connect, create, and celebrate. Embracing imperfection allows us to let go of the need for flawless execution, allowing for spontaneity, authenticity, and a more relaxed experience.

1. **Focus on Meaning Over Aesthetics**: Rather than striving for a picture-perfect holiday, focus on creating meaningful experiences. Whether it's decorating, gift-giving, or preparing a holiday meal, prioritize activities that feel joyful and meaningful over those that simply look impressive. This shift in perspective helps to reduce the pressure to create a flawless image and allows you to experience the season more fully.
2. **Create Your Own Traditions**: Often, perfectionism is tied to external expectations or comparisons with others. By creating personal holiday traditions that reflect your values, interests, and lifestyle, you can step away from the pressure to conform to societal standards. Unique traditions bring a sense of ownership and joy, allowing you to celebrate in a way that feels true to yourself.
3. **Embrace Spontaneity**: Perfectionism often leads us to over-plan, seeking to control every aspect of the holiday experience. Embracing spontaneity and

flexibility allows room for unexpected moments of joy and connection. Imperfections, surprises, and even minor mishaps are often the moments we remember most fondly, adding richness and authenticity to the holiday experience.
4. **Practice Self-Compassion**: Remember that it's okay to have an imperfect holiday season. Practicing self-compassion means acknowledging that your worth is not defined by the quality of your decorations, the size of your gatherings, or the gifts you give. Letting go of perfectionism involves recognizing that your presence, kindness, and thoughtfulness are what truly make the holiday special.

Managing the Pressures of Social Media and Comparison

Social media can intensify feelings of inadequacy and amplify perfectionistic tendencies during the holidays. While it can be a source of inspiration, it also creates a constant opportunity for comparison, leading to feelings of envy, inadequacy, and dissatisfaction. Managing social media pressures requires a mindful approach, allowing us to engage with the season in a way that feels genuine and centered.

1. **Limit Social Media Consumption**: Consider setting boundaries around your social media use during the holidays. Designate certain times to check social media or limit your usage to specific days. Taking breaks from social media can help reduce the temptation to compare and allow you to be more present in your own experiences.
2. **Curate Your Feed**: Surround yourself with content that aligns with your values and promotes positivity,

authenticity, and self-acceptance. Unfollow accounts that trigger feelings of inadequacy or create pressure to conform to unrealistic standards. Curating your feed helps to create a more supportive online environment that reflects the values you hold for the holiday season.
3. **Engage Mindfully**: If you do choose to share your holiday moments on social media, do so with intention. Focus on sharing meaningful experiences rather than seeking validation or approval. Remember that your holiday experience is not a performance and that its value lies in personal joy, connection, and fulfillment rather than external validation.
4. **Reflect on Gratitude**: Practicing gratitude can help to shift your focus from what's missing to what you have. By regularly reflecting on the aspects of your life and holiday experience that bring joy and fulfillment, you can cultivate a sense of contentment that transcends comparison. Gratitude helps to ground us in our unique experiences, reminding us that true joy comes from within.

Reclaiming the holidays is about setting boundaries, embracing imperfection, and resisting the pull of societal expectations and comparisons. By establishing healthy boundaries with family and friends, we can protect our mental health, honor our needs, and create a holiday season that feels manageable and meaningful. Avoiding the trap of comparison and perfectionism allows us to celebrate with authenticity, focusing on the experiences and connections that truly matter.

In the following chapters, we will explore practical tools for incorporating mindfulness and self-care into your holiday routine, helping you to cultivate a season of balance, joy, and renewal. By approaching the holidays with intention, self-awareness, and a commitment to well-being, you can create a holiday experience that feels enriching, fulfilling, and true to yourself.

Chapter 3
Cultivating Mindfulness and Present Moment Awareness

In the rush of holiday activities, we often find ourselves moving from one event to the next, our minds filled with checklists and obligations rather than true presence. This lack of presence can make even the most joyful experiences feel rushed, leaving us with little time to savor the moments that make the season special. Mindfulness, the practice of being fully present in each moment, offers a powerful antidote to holiday stress and busyness. By incorporating mindfulness into our holiday traditions and creating intentional moments of pause, we can experience the season with a sense of calm, joy, and connection. This chapter explores practical ways to cultivate mindfulness during the holidays, from mindful eating and present-moment awareness in gatherings to simple practices that bring peace to busy holiday days.

Integrating Mindfulness into Holiday Traditions

The holidays are filled with sensory experiences that lend themselves beautifully to mindfulness—the warmth of a gathering, the taste of a holiday meal, the colors of decorations, and the sounds of festive music. Yet, amid the excitement, it's easy to slip into autopilot, missing these moments as we focus on planning, organizing, and checking off tasks. Integrating mindfulness into holiday traditions allows us to engage with these moments fully, creating richer experiences and a deeper appreciation for the season. In this section, we'll explore how to bring mindfulness into two key aspects of holiday traditions: eating and gatherings.

Mindful Eating During Holiday Meals

Food plays a central role in holiday traditions, often symbolizing love, connection, and culture. However, the abundance of food during this season can lead to mindless eating, where we consume quickly and without intention. Mindful eating, the practice of savoring each bite and being fully present in the experience of eating, not only enhances our enjoyment of holiday meals but also promotes better digestion and helps us make conscious choices about what and how much we eat.

1. **Engage Your Senses**: Begin by taking a moment to observe your food—the colors, textures, aromas, and presentation. Engaging your senses before eating brings your focus to the present moment and prepares your body for digestion. As you take each bite, savor the flavors and textures, noticing how the food feels and tastes.
2. **Eat Slowly and Chew Thoroughly**: Eating slowly allows you to truly savor the meal and provides

time for your body to signal when it's full. Chewing thoroughly also aids in digestion and enhances the eating experience. Take pauses between bites to check in with your hunger and fullness levels, allowing you to eat with intention rather than automatically.
3. **Express Gratitude**: Before or during your meal, take a moment to reflect on the people, traditions, and efforts behind the food on your plate. Whether it's a family recipe passed down through generations or a dish prepared by a loved one, acknowledging the source of your food cultivates gratitude and deepens your connection to the meal.
4. **Honor Your Body's Needs**: The abundance of holiday treats can make it tempting to indulge beyond our comfort levels. Practicing mindful eating doesn't mean restriction; rather, it's about honoring your body's needs and making choices that feel nourishing and satisfying. Listen to your body's cues, and remember that enjoying holiday foods mindfully is part of the celebration.

Staying Present in Gatherings and Activities

Holiday gatherings bring opportunities for connection, laughter, and shared joy. However, it's easy to become distracted, whether by our phones, our thoughts, or our to-do lists, and miss out on fully connecting with others. Practicing presence in gatherings allows us to be truly engaged, creating memories that are rich in connection and meaning.

1. **Be Fully Engaged**: When engaging in conversation, focus on the person you're speaking with rather than letting your mind wander or checking your

phone. Listen actively, make eye contact, and be genuinely interested in their words. This mindful approach not only enhances the quality of your interactions but also shows respect and care for the people around you.
2. **Practice Non-Judgmental Awareness**: Family gatherings can sometimes bring up challenging emotions or conflicts. Practicing non-judgmental awareness allows you to observe these emotions without reacting impulsively. Notice your feelings, accept them, and allow them to pass rather than letting them control your responses. This approach creates a calm, grounded presence, helping you navigate social dynamics with ease and kindness.
3. **Create Rituals of Reflection**: Take time during gatherings to reflect on the moment. You might pause to look around the room, notice the faces of loved ones, or listen to the sounds of laughter and conversation. These moments of quiet reflection help to anchor you in the present, enhancing your appreciation for the gathering and the connections within it.
4. **Savor Shared Experiences**: Whether it's a family tradition, a game, or a group activity, approach shared experiences with a spirit of curiosity and enjoyment. Instead of focusing on the outcome or perfection, immerse yourself in the process. By savoring the experience as it unfolds, you create memories that are rooted in joy and connection rather than stress or expectation.

Integrating mindfulness into holiday traditions allows us to experience the season with greater depth and connection, making each moment feel rich with meaning and presence. Through mindful eating and present-moment awareness in gatherings, we cultivate a sense of gratitude, fulfillment, and authenticity that enhances our holiday experience.

Creating Moments of Pause

Amid the busyness of the holidays, finding moments of pause can feel like a challenge. However, these brief respites are essential for maintaining mental and emotional well-being. Moments of pause allow us to reset, recharge, and return to the present with a clear mind and a calm spirit. Simple mindfulness practices—such as breathing exercises, meditation, and reflection—can be woven into even the busiest days, helping us to navigate the season with balance and tranquility. This section explores practical techniques for creating moments of pause, offering tools that bring peace to the holiday rush.

Simple Mindfulness Practices for Busy Holiday Days

Even on the busiest days, mindfulness practices can create a sense of calm and presence, allowing us to approach the holidays with a centered mindset. These practices are simple, accessible, and can be done in just a few minutes, making them ideal for busy holiday schedules.

1. **The 5-4-3-2-1 Grounding Exercise**: This quick grounding exercise uses your senses to bring you into the present moment. Wherever you are, identify five things you can see, four things you can touch, three things you can hear, two things you can smell, and one thing you can taste. This exercise quickly redirects

your focus from stress or distractions to the present, creating a sense of calm and clarity.
2. **Mindful Transitions**: Use moments of transition—such as moving from one room to another, sitting down for a meal, or arriving at a gathering—as opportunities for mindfulness. Take a deep breath, set an intention for the moment ahead, and arrive fully present. This small practice helps to keep you grounded, making each transition a mindful pause rather than a rushed shift.
3. **Body Scan**: A body scan involves bringing awareness to different parts of your body, noticing any sensations, tension, or relaxation. Begin at your toes and slowly move up to the top of your head, observing each area without judgment. The body scan can be done in just a few minutes and is especially helpful for releasing physical tension and promoting relaxation.

Breathing Exercises, Meditation, and Reflection

Breathing exercises, meditation, and moments of reflection are powerful mindfulness tools that can bring a sense of peace to even the most hectic holiday days. These practices help us to slow down, connect with our inner selves, and return to the present moment with a sense of balance and clarity.

1. **Deep Breathing Exercise**: Deep breathing activates the body's relaxation response, reducing stress and promoting calm. Try the 4-7-8 breathing technique: inhale for a count of four, hold for a count of seven, and exhale for a count of eight. Repeat this cycle several times, allowing your breath to become a calming anchor that steadies your mind and body.

2. **Meditation**: A short meditation can create a moment of stillness in a busy day, helping you to reconnect with yourself. Find a quiet space, close your eyes, and focus on your breath. If your mind begins to wander, gently bring your attention back to your breath. Even a five-minute meditation can bring a sense of peace, grounding you in the present and allowing you to approach the day with greater clarity.
3. **Reflective Journaling**: Set aside a few minutes each day to journal your thoughts, feelings, or reflections. Journaling provides an outlet for processing emotions and clarifying intentions. You might reflect on what you're grateful for, record a meaningful moment from the day, or write down a positive intention for the days ahead. These reflections create a sense of mindfulness and gratitude, helping you to stay connected to what matters most during the holidays.
4. **Loving-Kindness Meditation**: Loving-kindness meditation is a practice of directing compassion toward yourself and others. Begin by offering kind thoughts to yourself, such as "May I be happy, may I be healthy, may I be peaceful." Then extend these wishes to loved ones, acquaintances, and even those you may have conflicts with. This practice fosters compassion, reduces stress, and enhances your sense of connection, allowing you to approach the holidays with a loving and open heart.

Embracing Moments of Quiet

Amid holiday festivities, moments of quiet can be profoundly restorative. Whether it's a walk in nature, a moment of silence by a lit candle, or simply sitting in stillness, these quiet moments create a space for introspection, grounding, and renewal. Embracing moments of quiet allows us to find balance, helping us to recharge and enter each holiday activity with a sense of calm and centeredness.

Cultivating mindfulness and present-moment awareness during the holidays transforms each experience into a source of joy, connection, and calm. By integrating mindfulness into holiday traditions—such as eating mindfully and staying present in gatherings—we can fully engage in the season, creating memories that are rich in meaning and connection. Creating moments of pause, through breathing exercises, meditation, and reflection, allows us to find balance and peace amid the holiday rush.

In the chapters to come, we will explore additional tools for fostering mental, emotional, and physical wellness during the holidays. By approaching the season with a mindful, present, and intentional mindset, you can reclaim the holidays as a time of renewal, creating a holiday experience that nourishes your spirit and prepares you for the year ahead.

Chapter 4
Self-Care Rituals for the Holiday Season

The holiday season is a time for giving, sharing, and celebrating, but in the midst of tending to others, our own needs can easily become an afterthought. Practicing self-care is essential for navigating the holidays with resilience and joy, helping us stay grounded, energized, and connected to ourselves amid the demands of the season. True self-care goes beyond pampering or indulgence; it's about fostering a sense of well-being and honoring our mental, emotional, and physical needs. This chapter explores self-care practices for the holidays, from small, daily rituals to strategies for cultivating self-compassion, providing a foundation for a season that feels balanced, nurturing, and sustainable.

Daily Self-Care Practices

With holiday schedules packed with events, gatherings, and preparations, finding time for self-care can feel like an impossible task. Yet, self-care doesn't need to be time-consuming or complex to be effective. Small, simple rituals practiced daily can make a significant difference, helping us to stay centered and connected to ourselves even on the busiest days. This section provides ideas for integrating self-care into daily routines, along with guidance on creating a personalized self-care plan that fits seamlessly into holiday schedules.

Embracing Small, Doable Rituals

Self-care rituals don't need to be elaborate or lengthy to have a meaningful impact. In fact, small acts of self-care can be more sustainable and easier to incorporate into holiday routines. The key is to identify practices that nourish your mind, body, and spirit, creating moments of calm and joy amid the season's busyness. Here are some small, doable self-care rituals that can easily fit into your day:

1. **Journaling**: Writing down your thoughts, reflections, or feelings can provide a mental release, helping you to process emotions and gain clarity. Even a few minutes of journaling each day can be grounding, allowing you to start or end your day with a sense of mindfulness. Consider writing down three things you're grateful for, setting an intention for the day, or reflecting on a meaningful moment from the day's events.
2. **Walking or Movement**: Physical movement is one of the most effective ways to relieve stress and elevate

your mood. A short walk, gentle stretching, or even a quick dance break can be a refreshing form of self-care. Aim to take breaks for movement throughout the day, particularly during moments of high stress or after long periods of sitting. Walking in nature, if possible, can add an extra layer of calm and rejuvenation.

3. **Reading**: Setting aside time to read something you enjoy, whether it's a novel, a poem, or an inspiring article, can be a soothing ritual that transports you away from the holiday rush. Even ten minutes of reading before bed or during a quiet moment can help you relax and refocus.

4. **Morning or Evening Rituals**: Creating a small morning or evening ritual can set a positive tone for the day ahead or help you unwind at night. This might include lighting a candle, listening to soothing music, practicing a few minutes of deep breathing, or simply taking a few moments to sit quietly. Establishing a ritual that you can rely on every day provides a sense of consistency and grounding amid the fluctuations of the holiday season.

5. **Breathwork and Mini Meditations**: Short breathing exercises and mini-meditations can be powerful tools for managing stress, and they require only a few minutes of time. Simple practices, such as taking five deep breaths or closing your eyes for a quick mindfulness check-in, can instantly create a sense of calm and reset your focus. Incorporating these moments throughout your day can keep you balanced, no matter how busy the day becomes.

Creating a Personal Self-Care Plan

Developing a self-care plan can help you prioritize self-care even on the most hectic days. Your self-care plan should be realistic, personalized, and adaptable to your holiday schedule. Here are some tips for creating a plan that aligns with your needs and fits within the season:

1. **Assess Your Needs**: Begin by identifying the areas where you need the most support. Are you looking to manage stress, maintain energy, or find moments of solitude? Knowing your specific needs can guide you in choosing self-care practices that will be most beneficial.
2. **Set Priorities**: Given the time constraints of the season, it's important to prioritize certain practices over others. Identify two or three self-care activities that are most meaningful to you and commit to incorporating them daily. For example, if movement is essential for managing stress, prioritize a daily walk or stretch session.
3. **Integrate Self-Care into Existing Routines**: Rather than adding new activities, try weaving self-care into routines you already have. For instance, if you drink tea or coffee in the morning, use that time for a few moments of mindful breathing or gratitude reflection. Small adjustments can make self-care feel natural and achievable.
4. **Create Flexible Options**: Some days may be busier than others, so it's helpful to have flexible self-care options. For example, if you can't go for a 30-minute walk, take a five-minute stretch break instead. Having both "long" and "short" versions of your self-care practices ensures that you can still engage in self-care, even on your busiest days.

5. **Schedule Breaks and Set Boundaries**:
   Protecting your time is a form of self-care. Set boundaries around certain times of day when you'll take a break, recharge, or practice self-care. This might mean reserving the first 15 minutes of the morning for yourself or taking a short break in the afternoon. Scheduling these moments can help prevent burnout and keep you feeling balanced.

Daily self-care practices don't require significant time or effort, but they provide essential support for managing holiday stress. By embracing small rituals and creating a personal self-care plan, you can nurture your well-being throughout the season, ensuring that you remain grounded, energized, and connected to yourself.

Self-Compassion Over Perfection

The holiday season is often steeped in the desire to create perfect experiences—for ourselves, for our loved ones, and for those around us. This pursuit of perfection, however, can lead to unrealistic expectations, guilt, and stress, detracting from the joy and authenticity of the season. Practicing self-compassion allows us to release these pressures, embracing a more forgiving and gentle approach toward ourselves. In this section, we'll explore the power of self-compassion, offering guidance on how to be kind to yourself in moments of stress, let go of guilt, and manage unrealistic expectations during the holidays.

Practicing Kindness Towards Yourself in Moments of Stress

Self-compassion, at its core, is the practice of treating ourselves with the same kindness, care, and understanding that we would offer to a friend. During the holidays, when stress levels can run high, practicing self-compassion helps to soften our inner critic and provide a sense of comfort in difficult moments. Here are some strategies for cultivating self-compassion during the season:

1. **Acknowledge Your Feelings**: The first step to self-compassion is acknowledging and validating your emotions, even if they're not what you expect or want to feel. Whether you're feeling overwhelmed, stressed, or disappointed, give yourself permission to feel these emotions without judgment. Self-compassion involves accepting yourself as you are, emotions and all.
2. **Speak Kindly to Yourself**: Notice the language you use toward yourself, particularly in moments of stress or perceived failure. If you catch yourself being self-critical, pause and reframe your inner dialogue with kindness and encouragement. For example, instead of saying, "I should have done better," try, "I did my best with what I had, and that's enough."
3. **Practice the "Self-Compassion Break"**: The self-compassion break is a technique developed by psychologist Kristin Neff, which involves taking a moment to recognize your feelings, remind yourself that everyone experiences stress, and offer yourself comforting words. This practice can be particularly helpful during stressful holiday moments, providing a quick way to reset and show yourself kindness.
4. **Treat Yourself with the Kindness of a Friend**: Imagine what you would say to a friend who was feeling stressed, overwhelmed, or disappointed. Now, offer those same words of encouragement to yourself. Self-compassion encourages us to shift our

perspective, viewing ourselves with warmth, understanding, and care.

Managing Guilt and Letting Go of Unrealistic Expectations

Holiday perfectionism is often fueled by unrealistic expectations and an internal pressure to meet certain standards. When we inevitably fall short of these ideals, guilt can arise, leaving us feeling inadequate or disappointed. Practicing self-compassion helps us to release these burdens, allowing us to approach the holidays with a mindset of acceptance and authenticity.

1. **Reframe Expectations**: Identify any unrealistic expectations you may be holding onto, whether it's about creating the perfect gathering, giving the perfect gifts, or meeting every social obligation. Remind yourself that perfection is neither achievable nor necessary. By reframing these expectations, you can create a holiday experience that is both enjoyable and sustainable.

2. **Embrace Imperfection as Part of the Journey**: Holidays are rarely flawless, and that's part of what makes them memorable. Embrace imperfections, mishaps, and changes as part of the holiday experience. By letting go of the need for everything to be "just right," you open yourself up to unexpected joys and a more relaxed, authentic celebration.

3. **Release the "Shoulds" and Focus on the "Coulds"**: The language of "should" often leads to guilt, as it implies obligation and expectation. Try replacing "should" with "could" or "want to," shifting from a mindset of pressure to one of possibility. For

example, instead of thinking, "I should attend every event," you might reframe it as, "I could attend a few events that feel meaningful to me."

4. **Forgive Yourself for Past "Mistakes"**: Sometimes, holiday guilt arises from past experiences or perceived "failures." Practicing self-forgiveness allows you to release these burdens, recognizing that everyone makes mistakes and that each holiday is an opportunity to create new memories. Self-forgiveness cultivates a sense of freedom and peace, enabling you to approach the season with an open heart.
5. **Prioritize What Matters Most**: Rather than spreading yourself thin trying to do everything, identify what truly matters to you this holiday season. Focus on the people, activities, and moments that bring you joy and fulfillment. By prioritizing what's meaningful, you can let go of guilt over not doing "enough" and create a holiday experience that aligns with your values.

Self-compassion over perfection is a transformative approach that allows us to embrace the holiday season with kindness, patience, and authenticity. By practicing kindness towards ourselves, managing guilt, and letting go of unrealistic expectations, we can experience a holiday that feels more relaxed, joyful, and aligned with our true selves.

Self-care and self-compassion are essential components of a balanced, fulfilling holiday season. Daily self-care practices provide moments of renewal and grounding, helping us to stay connected to ourselves amid the holiday rush. Embracing self-compassion allows us to release the burdens of guilt and perfectionism, creating space for a more authentic and joyful holiday experience.

In the chapters to come, we will delve into additional strategies for managing holiday stress, fostering meaningful connections, and creating a holiday season that honors your well-being and personal values. By incorporating self-care and self-compassion into your holiday journey, you can navigate the season with resilience, grace, and a sense of inner peace, setting the foundation for a truly nourishing holiday experience.

Chapter 5
Nutrition and Physical Wellness During the Holidays

The holiday season invites us into a world of flavors, aromas, and beloved family recipes, turning gatherings into feasts for the senses. This time of year brings with it the temptation to indulge, as shared meals and seasonal treats take center stage in our celebrations. Yet, the richness of holiday foods need not compromise our well-being. Embracing a balanced approach allows us to enjoy the season's culinary delights while nourishing our bodies and maintaining our energy levels.

Balanced Nutrition and Mindful Indulgence

The holiday season brings a wave of traditions, gatherings, and festivities. For many, it's a time marked by sharing meals, treats, and indulging in family favorites. While food is a central part of the holidays, maintaining a balance between indulgence and nutrition can help keep energy levels stable and improve mood, leaving you feeling better overall.

Enjoying Holiday Treats Without Overindulgence

Holiday meals are meant to be enjoyed, and there's no need to deny yourself the treats and dishes you love. With a mindful approach, it's possible to enjoy these foods without falling into the pitfalls of overindulgence. Here are some practical ways to do so:

1 Start with Smaller Portions: Begin with smaller servings, especially for richer or calorie-dense foods. Not only does this allow you to sample everything, but it also gives your body time to process the flavors and textures, helping you recognize when you're satisfied.

2 Prioritize Your Favorites: The holiday table often offers an abundance of options, some of which may not be particularly meaningful to you. Prioritizing dishes that hold sentimental value or that you genuinely enjoy helps prevent overeating foods you aren't truly interested in.

3 Slow Down: Savor each bite and take time to enjoy the taste, smell, and texture of your food. Eating more slowly not only enhances the experience but also gives your body time to signal fullness, reducing the likelihood of overeating.

4 Stay Hydrated: It's easy to mistake thirst for hunger, especially with holiday cocktails and rich foods in abundance. Drinking water regularly can help keep you hydrated and avoid the urge to overeat due to dehydration.

5 Balance the Plate: Alongside holiday favorites, aim to include nutrient-rich foods that keep you feeling fuller for longer. Filling half of your plate with vegetables, for example, provides vitamins, minerals, and fiber that support digestion and energy levels.

Mindful Eating Tips for Maintaining Energy and Mood

Mindful eating goes beyond simply limiting portions; it emphasizes awareness, enjoyment, and appreciation of the food we consume. Here are some mindful eating practices that can help maintain energy and a positive mood:

- **Check in with Hunger Levels**: Before reaching for seconds, pause and consider whether you're truly hungry. Tuning into physical hunger cues versus emotional or habitual eating can help prevent overeating.
- **Recognize Emotional Eating**: The holidays can bring up a range of emotions, from joy to nostalgia to stress. If you find yourself eating to manage these feelings, pause and consider other ways to cope, such as journaling, talking with a friend, or engaging in a soothing activity.
- **Focus on Your Company, Not Just Your Plate**: Eating mindfully is also about being present with the people around you. Engage in conversation, share stories, and let the social aspects of the holiday table enrich your experience. Eating in this way can make each meal more fulfilling without overreliance on the food itself for satisfaction.
- **Be Kind to Yourself**: If you do overindulge, avoid self-criticism. Allowing yourself the grace to enjoy the holidays without guilt will enable you to bounce back, refocus, and avoid falling into restrictive eating patterns or cycles of guilt.

Balancing nutrition with indulgence during the holidays isn't about rigid restrictions but rather thoughtful moderation and self-awareness. By listening to your body's cues and making conscious choices, you can celebrate without feeling deprived or overindulged.

Incorporating Gentle Movement

Amid the busyness of the holiday season, physical activity is often one of the first routines to fall by the wayside. However, movement is vital for maintaining wellness, especially during a season that can be both physically and mentally demanding. Incorporating gentle, enjoyable activities helps sustain energy, manage stress, and keep you feeling good.

Finding Joy in Physical Activities

Holiday physical activity doesn't need to be intense. The key is to find movement that feels enjoyable rather than burdensome. Here are some ways to incorporate gentle, joy-filled activity:

1 Take Morning Walks: Starting your day with a brisk walk outdoors is a wonderful way to set a positive tone for the day, clear your mind, and energize your body. If possible, invite a family member or friend along to make it a social activity.

2 Explore Yoga or Stretching Routines: Yoga or simple stretching routines can provide both mental relaxation and physical benefits. Gentle stretching can reduce muscle tension and increase flexibility, helping combat the stiffness that can result from prolonged sitting at gatherings.

3 Dance: Dancing, whether by yourself or with family and friends, is a fantastic way to stay active. It doesn't feel like exercise, yet it gets your heart rate up, improves mood, and creates enjoyable memories.

4 Mindful Movement: Incorporate simple, mindful movements into your day. For example, taking a few minutes to focus on breathing and perform some gentle stretching between activities or events can re-center your focus and bring relief from any tension or stress.

Creating New Holiday Traditions that Promote Movement and Connection

Another effective way to incorporate movement is by making it a part of your holiday traditions. Introducing fun, activity-based traditions encourages everyone to join in and creates shared experiences beyond sitting down for meals. Here are some ideas for starting activity-based traditions:

• **Family Walks Post-Meal**: Going for a walk after a holiday meal allows everyone to digest and enjoy the crisp air. This can be especially refreshing in the evenings, with holiday lights and decorations adding to the charm.

• **Active Games**: Incorporate active games like charades, scavenger hunts, or dance-offs into family gatherings. These activities encourage everyone to move and bring out laughter and light-heartedness.

• **Holiday-Themed Races or Events**: Many communities host holiday-themed fun runs or charity walks. Participating in one of these as a family or group can turn it into an annual tradition that combines movement with community engagement and giving back.

• **Home Workouts with Family**: Short, light workouts done together can be a fun bonding experience. From simple bodyweight exercises to yoga routines, sharing movement as a family can be fun and beneficial for everyone.

Introducing gentle movement into your holiday routine

doesn't have to be about fitness goals or exertion but rather about creating moments of joy, connection, and physical activity that help balance out the season's indulgent foods and sedentary gatherings.

The Stress-Free Holiday Wellness Guide: Mindful Self-Care and Int...

The holidays can be a time to savor good food, indulge in beloved treats, and connect with loved ones. By approaching holiday nutrition with a balance of mindful indulgence and nutritious choices, it's possible to enjoy every bite without feeling deprived or overly indulgent. Coupling these practices with gentle, enjoyable movement enriches both physical and emotional wellness, keeping stress at bay and energy levels steady.

Incorporating mindfulness in both nutrition and movement creates a holiday experience that is fulfilling, healthy, and genuinely enjoyable. Embracing this balanced approach to wellness during the holidays allows you to make the most of the season, ensuring that you feel rejuvenated and centered rather than drained or regretful. In doing so, you not only nourish your body and mind but also build lasting traditions that enhance the joy and meaning of the holiday season year after year.

Chapter 6
Social Connections: Fostering Healthy Relationships

The holiday season is a time when relationships take center stage, with family gatherings, social events, and meaningful connections becoming focal points of celebration. However, the quality of these interactions often varies, and for many, holiday gatherings can be emotionally complex, amplifying stress and tension. Fostering healthy relationships during this season requires intentionality, focusing on quality interactions, and navigating family dynamics with patience and realistic expectations. This chapter delves into strategies for creating meaningful interactions, strengthening communication, and managing family dynamics to cultivate a harmonious and fulfilling holiday experience.

Creating Meaningful Interactions

In a season filled with social gatherings and traditions, prioritizing quality over quantity in interactions can make a significant difference in emotional fulfillment. Shifting focus from attending every event to creating depth in chosen gatherings can result in connections that feel genuine and supportive. This section explores how to cultivate meaningful interactions through intentional communication and presence, providing tools for deepening connections and reducing conflicts.

Focusing on Quality Over Quantity in Holiday Gatherings

Attending numerous gatherings often leads to social burnout, leaving little room for meaningful connections. Quality interactions involve choosing gatherings that resonate personally and allow for more authentic engagement. Here's how to focus on meaningful interactions:

1. **Prioritize Intentional Gatherings**: Rather than accepting every invitation, focus on gatherings where you feel comfortable and connected to the people involved. Prioritize events that foster genuine connection over those driven by obligation. Smaller gatherings can facilitate deeper conversations, allowing for more meaningful exchanges.

2. **Engage in Active Listening**: In conversations, practice active listening—fully focusing on the speaker, asking thoughtful questions, and showing genuine interest in their words. Active listening enhances the quality of communication and builds trust, making interactions more fulfilling and less prone to misunderstandings.
3. **Seek Depth in Conversations**: Rather than staying on surface-level topics, consider gently guiding conversations toward meaningful subjects. Asking open-ended questions such as, "What's been most meaningful to you this year?" encourages reflection and openness, fostering a sense of closeness and understanding.
4. **Limit Distractions**: To maximize the quality of interactions, minimize distractions, particularly from phones or external interruptions. Give full attention to those you're with to cultivate an atmosphere of respect and presence. This undivided attention can deepen relationships and create memorable, rewarding interactions.

Communication Strategies to Deepen Connections and Reduce Conflict

Effective communication is key to meaningful connections and plays a vital role in preventing conflicts. Clear, compassionate communication fosters openness and respect, while conflict management strategies help navigate sensitive situations. Here's how to use communication to strengthen bonds during the holidays:

1. **Use "I" Statements**: Communicating with "I" statements instead of "you" statements can make a

significant difference in expressing feelings without assigning blame. For example, "I feel overwhelmed when we discuss politics" conveys your feelings without accusing others, reducing defensiveness and promoting understanding.

2. **Establish Clear Boundaries**: Setting boundaries—whether regarding sensitive topics, personal space, or time limits—supports mutual respect and clarity. Communicate boundaries calmly and directly, such as saying, "I'd love to catch up, but I have a limited time." Boundaries prevent misunderstandings and help maintain emotional balance.

3. **Practice Empathy**: Empathy is essential in cultivating genuine connections and navigating conflicts. When faced with a disagreement, take a moment to consider the other person's perspective, even if you don't agree. This practice can defuse tension and allow for a more productive, respectful conversation.

4. **De-escalate Conflict with a Pause**: When tensions rise, taking a brief pause can prevent arguments from escalating. Excuse yourself for a moment if necessary, taking a few deep breaths or stepping outside to regain composure. Returning to the conversation with calmness often allows for more constructive communication.

5. **Express Appreciation**: Acknowledging others' presence, kindness, or support can make interactions more positive and meaningful. Expressing appreciation creates a foundation of warmth and connection, making gatherings feel supportive and welcoming, even amid differences.

Creating meaningful interactions is about intentionality, choosing quality over quantity, and using communication as a tool to deepen connections. By prioritizing present, respectful, and empathetic engagement, you can create fulfilling holiday experiences that nourish relationships and foster a sense of belonging.

Navigating Family Dynamics

Family dynamics during the holidays can bring both joy and stress, particularly in situations with longstanding conflicts, differing viewpoints, or emotional sensitivities. Navigating these dynamics requires setting realistic expectations, preparing for potential triggers, and employing strategies that promote peace and understanding. This section provides guidance on managing challenging family interactions, setting healthy boundaries, and approaching family gatherings with a balanced, grounded mindset.

Tips for Reducing Tension in Potentially Difficult Family Situations

Tension in family gatherings can arise from unresolved conflicts, personality clashes, or sensitive topics. Managing these situations proactively can help reduce friction and create a more harmonious environment.

1. **Prepare Mentally**: Anticipate potential challenges and practice self-regulation techniques before gatherings. If certain topics or individuals are known to trigger stress, have a plan for staying calm, such as grounding yourself with deep breathing or focusing on positive intentions. Being prepared reduces reactivity and allows you to approach situations with composure.
2. **Set Topic Boundaries**: If certain discussions (like politics or personal decisions) often lead to tension, setting boundaries around these topics can protect

your peace. Politely steering conversations away from sensitive subjects or calmly stating that you prefer not to discuss them can prevent conflicts before they start.
3. **Use Humor to Defuse Tension**: Light humor can diffuse tension and keep interactions relaxed. When a conversation becomes heated, a gentle joke or lighthearted comment can redirect the focus and prevent escalation. This technique works best when humor is used tactfully, respecting everyone's feelings and keeping the atmosphere friendly.
4. **Designate a "Safe Space" Partner**: Identify a trusted family member or friend who understands your needs and can serve as a source of support if tension arises. Check in with each other throughout the gathering, offering mutual encouragement and, if needed, a quick escape from stressful conversations.
5. **Practice Non-Reactivity**: Choosing not to react to provocative comments or criticisms can prevent situations from escalating. If someone makes a comment intended to provoke, consider responding with neutrality or redirecting the conversation. Remaining calm and non-reactive often takes the wind out of confrontational interactions.

Setting Realistic Expectations for Family Interactions

Many holiday disappointments stem from unrealistic expectations. Families are often complex, and holiday gatherings may not always go as planned. Setting realistic expectations helps to approach gatherings with acceptance and flexibility, making it easier to navigate imperfections with grace.

1. **Accept Family Members as They Are**: Recognize that family members may not change or behave as you would like them to. Accepting them as they are allows you to approach interactions without expecting them to align with your preferences or ideals, reducing frustration and disappointment.
2. **Focus on Moments of Connection**: Rather than expecting every interaction to be perfect, focus on small moments of connection, such as a kind exchange or a shared laugh. Embracing these positive moments makes it easier to navigate the gathering without getting caught up in disappointments.
3. **Release the Need for Approval**: Family gatherings can stir up old dynamics, including the need for validation or approval. Remind yourself that your worth is not defined by others' opinions, freeing you to engage in interactions without trying to meet others' expectations. This mindset fosters a sense of inner peace and confidence.
4. **Acknowledge Your Emotional Boundaries**: Set boundaries for your emotional involvement in family dynamics. Be mindful of situations or discussions that drain your energy or provoke stress, and disengage as needed. Protecting your emotional boundaries allows you to interact with family from a balanced, resilient place.
5. **Embrace Flexibility**: Flexibility allows you to adapt to unexpected changes and imperfections. Family gatherings rarely unfold perfectly, and embracing flexibility helps you to stay calm and grounded amid surprises. Approaching the day with an open mind and flexible attitude creates a more enjoyable experience.

The Stress-Free Holiday Wellness Guide: Mindful Self-Care and Int...

Navigating family dynamics requires a balance of self-awareness, boundaries, and acceptance. By preparing mentally, setting topic boundaries, and managing expectations, you can reduce stress and approach gatherings with resilience, creating space for peaceful and fulfilling family interactions.

Fostering healthy relationships during the holidays means embracing both the joys and challenges of social connections. By prioritizing meaningful interactions and using communication to deepen connections, you can create holiday gatherings that feel rewarding and supportive. Navigating family dynamics with acceptance, boundaries, and realistic expectations allows for a holiday experience that honors both your well-being and the complexities of family relationships.

In the final chapters, we will explore ways to carry these relationship skills into the new year, building on the foundation of wellness and connection cultivated throughout the holiday season. Through meaningful connections, balanced family interactions, and authentic engagement, you can create a holiday experience that feels both harmonious and deeply satisfying, leaving you refreshed and renewed for the year ahead.

Chapter 7
Handling Grief and Loneliness During the Holidays

The holiday season, often associated with joy, family, and celebration, can feel particularly difficult for those dealing with grief or loneliness. The absence of loved ones, feelings of isolation, or the memories of past holidays can make this time of year feel bittersweet, if not overwhelming. However, navigating these feelings with intention and self-compassion can help transform the season into a period of healing, reflection, and even quiet joy. This chapter explores ways to acknowledge and honor loss while finding comfort and meaning in solitude, guiding you toward a more peaceful and fulfilling holiday experience.

Acknowledge and Honor Loss

Grieving the absence of loved ones during the holidays is a natural response to loss. This season often brings up memories and a longing for those who are no longer with us, making it essential to acknowledge these feelings openly rather than avoiding them. Honoring the lives and memories of loved ones can help maintain a sense of connection, allowing you to integrate their presence into your holiday season in meaningful ways. Here, we explore strategies for coping with grief during the holidays and ideas for honoring those who are no longer physically present.

Strategies for Coping with Grief During the Holidays

Managing grief during the holidays is a personal journey. While each experience is unique, here are some strategies to help you navigate this time with care and resilience:

1. **Give Yourself Permission to Feel**: Allow yourself to experience and express your emotions without guilt or judgment. Grief can come in waves, so it's natural to feel different emotions—sadness, longing, anger, or even moments of happiness—all at once. Acknowledging these feelings helps prevent them from becoming overwhelming and fosters a healthier approach to grief.
2. **Identify Emotional Triggers and Prepare for Them**: Certain traditions, songs, or moments may evoke memories or feelings of grief. Preparing for these triggers can help you manage them in real-time.

Plan ahead for potentially difficult moments and give yourself the option to take a break or adjust your involvement if needed.
3. **Set Boundaries for Social Gatherings**: The pressure to attend gatherings may feel particularly challenging when grieving. Remember, it's okay to say no or to leave early if events feel emotionally taxing. Communicate your needs to loved ones so they can support you in navigating these boundaries.
4. **Create Moments of Quiet Reflection**: Grieving often requires solitude and introspection, so intentionally carving out quiet moments can provide space for reflection. Spend time journaling, meditating, or simply sitting with your thoughts to process your emotions and honor your memories.
5. **Seek Support if Needed**: Consider speaking with friends, family members, or a support group that understands your experience. The simple act of talking about your feelings with others who have faced similar challenges can offer comfort, and sharing memories of your loved ones can keep their presence alive within your community.

Ways to Honor Loved Ones Who Are No Longer Present

Honoring loved ones during the holidays can be a meaningful way to feel connected to them, fostering a sense of presence and remembrance. Here are ways to bring their memory into your holiday traditions:

1. **Light a Candle in Their Memory**: Lighting a candle for a loved one can create a quiet moment of connection. You might choose a specific time each day

to light it, using that moment to reflect on the joy they brought into your life.
2. **Cook or Share Their Favorite Recipe**: Food can be a powerful way to keep memories alive. Preparing a loved one's favorite holiday dish or treat can feel comforting and meaningful. If you're gathering with others, share stories about them while you cook, bringing their spirit into the gathering.
3. **Create a Memory Ornament or Decoration**: Designing a holiday decoration that honors your loved one's memory, whether it's an ornament, wreath, or small display, can be a creative way to celebrate their life. This tradition becomes a visible reminder of their presence each year, blending memory with celebration.
4. **Write a Letter to Them**: Writing a letter to a loved one who has passed can be a therapeutic way to express feelings, share memories, or update them on your life. Place the letter somewhere meaningful, keep it in a journal, or even read it aloud in a quiet moment.
5. **Include Their Memory in Your Traditions**: You might honor your loved one by including their favorite traditions or activities in your holiday plans. Whether it's playing a favorite song, visiting a special place, or enjoying a ritual they loved, these acts of remembrance help create a sense of ongoing connection.

Acknowledge that grief is a complex journey, and creating ways to honor your loved ones can make the holiday season feel more supportive and meaningful. Celebrating their memory through intentional actions allows you to keep their spirit present, even as you navigate the changes that come with loss.

Finding Comfort in Solitude

Spending the holidays alone can feel challenging, but solitude doesn't have to mean loneliness. When approached with care and intention, spending the season solo can be an opportunity to create fulfilling experiences, engage in personal reflection, and embrace new traditions. This section explores ways to make holidays enjoyable when alone and offers ideas for crafting meaningful solo traditions that can bring comfort and joy.

Ideas for Making Holidays Enjoyable When Spending Them Alone

When spending the holidays alone, finding comfort in the small, intentional moments can create a sense of peace and joy. Here are ideas to help make solo holidays feel enriching and personally fulfilling:

1. **Create a Cozy, Festive Environment**: Decorate your space in a way that feels festive and comforting to you. Adding small touches like string lights, a seasonal candle, or cozy blankets can create a warm and inviting atmosphere. Personalizing your environment can make your holiday feel special, even when celebrated alone.
2. **Prepare a Meal You Love**: Treat yourself to a delicious, comforting meal, whether it's a favorite dish or something new you've wanted to try. The process of cooking can be a soothing ritual, and taking time to enjoy the meal mindfully brings a sense of self-care and celebration to your day.
3. **Plan a "Day of Joy" for Yourself**: Dedicate a day to activities that bring you joy, such as watching favorite movies, reading, baking, or exploring a new hobby. Give yourself permission to focus on your own

happiness, creating a holiday that is personalized to your preferences.
4. **Connect Virtually with Loved Ones**: If you feel the need for connection, consider a virtual get-together with friends or family. A brief video call, virtual meal, or shared activity can add a touch of togetherness without requiring you to leave your space.
5. **Reflect and Set Intentions for the New Year**: Use this solo time to reflect on your year, write down your accomplishments, and set intentions for the upcoming year. Engaging in personal reflection can create a sense of peace and purpose, turning the holiday season into a meaningful period of renewal.

How to Create Fulfilling Solo Traditions and Experiences

Creating solo holiday traditions allows you to celebrate in ways that feel authentic and comforting. By embracing solitude with intention, you can establish meaningful rituals that make the holiday season a source of fulfillment. Here are some ideas for crafting personalized solo traditions:

1. **Plan a Holiday Movie Marathon**: Choose a selection of holiday movies or shows that make you feel cozy and uplifted, and dedicate an evening or day to watching them. Setting aside this time for relaxation and enjoyment can become a tradition that you look forward to each year.
2. **Write a Gratitude Letter to Yourself**: Reflect on your accomplishments, strengths, and resilience from the past year, and write a letter acknowledging and celebrating these qualities. Practicing self-

gratitude can cultivate a sense of inner peace and remind you of your own resilience.

3. **Create a Vision Board or Reflection Journal**: Reflect on your hopes and dreams for the upcoming year by creating a vision board or writing in a reflection journal. Setting goals and visualizing your future can help you approach the new year with optimism and clarity, turning the holiday into a time of personal growth.

4. **Make or Buy a Gift for Yourself**: Celebrate yourself by treating yourself to a small gift that brings you joy, comfort, or relaxation. Whether it's a new book, a cozy blanket, or something that represents a personal goal, giving yourself a gift is a way to honor self-love and appreciation.

5. **Volunteer or Give Back**: Engaging in acts of kindness, such as volunteering or giving to a cause, can add a profound sense of purpose to your holiday season. Helping others often brings a sense of connection and gratitude, reminding you of the power of compassion and generosity.

6. **Practice a Daily Gratitude or Mindfulness Ritual**: Establish a daily gratitude or mindfulness ritual where you reflect on things you're grateful for or simply practice presence in the moment. This tradition can bring calm, focus, and positivity, providing comfort even in solitude.

Spending the holidays alone can be an opportunity to connect with yourself in new ways. By creating fulfilling solo traditions, you transform solitude into a source of joy, giving your holiday season personal meaning and depth. These practices allow you to embrace this time as a period of renewal, discovery, and intentional celebration.

The Stress-Free Holiday Wellness Guide: Mindful Self-Care and Int...

Navigating grief and loneliness during the holidays can be challenging, but with self-compassion and thoughtful intention, you can shape this season into a time of healing, reflection, and connection—whether with others, your loved ones' memory, or yourself. By acknowledging and honoring your feelings of loss, you create space to remember and celebrate those who are no longer with you. Finding comfort in solitude can also offer a unique chance to engage in self-care, build meaningful solo traditions, and appreciate the peace that the holidays can bring.

Ultimately, this season can become one of inner growth and fulfillment. By honoring both your grief and the moments of joy you create, you allow yourself to embrace a balanced holiday experience that respects your emotional needs and nurtures your spirit.

Chapter 8
Unplugging and Recharging: Digital Detox for the Holidays

The holidays are a natural time for reflection, connection, and self-renewal, yet the ever-present allure of technology—whether through social media, streaming, or constant notifications—can detract from the richness of the season. While screens offer convenience and connection, an overreliance on them can lead to distraction, comparison, and even burnout. Practicing a digital detox allows us to focus on what truly matters, creating space to reconnect with loved ones and ourselves. This chapter explores strategies for limiting screen time and creating meaningful, tech-free traditions that foster connection, presence, and well-being.

Limiting Screen Time

Reducing screen time during the holidays doesn't mean giving up technology entirely but rather using it with intention to support our well-being. By setting boundaries around screen time and practicing mindful social media use, we can reclaim moments of peace, connect more authentically with loved ones, and make the holiday experience more fulfilling. Here, we'll explore strategies to limit technology dependence and use social media mindfully.

Strategies to Reduce Technology Dependence During the Holidays

Balancing the use of technology with moments of presence can help reduce stress, improve focus, and enhance our holiday experience. Here are some effective strategies for limiting screen time:

1. **Set Screen-Free Times**: Designate specific times of the day as screen-free, such as mornings, mealtimes, or evenings. By setting aside these windows for non-screen activities, you create space to engage in meaningful experiences and enjoy the present moment without distraction.
2. **Limit Notifications**: Constant notifications can disrupt focus and pull us back into the digital world. Consider temporarily turning off notifications for social media, emails, or non-essential apps. Limiting notifications helps to maintain a peaceful holiday atmosphere, reducing the urge to check your phone frequently.

3. **Create "Check-In" Windows for Social Media**: If staying connected on social media is important to you, consider setting designated times to check in, such as once in the morning and once in the evening. Having specific windows for social media allows you to enjoy its benefits while keeping it from overtaking your holiday experience.
4. **Use Physical Alternatives**: Instead of relying on digital calendars, lists, or reminders, try using a physical notebook or planner for holiday planning. Writing things down by hand can reduce screen dependency and create a more tangible, personal connection to your tasks and plans.
5. **Set App Time Limits**: Many smartphones allow you to set daily time limits for specific apps. Use these limits for social media, games, or other apps that tend to be time-consuming. When you reach the time limit, consider it a reminder to step away and engage in a non-digital activity that brings you joy.
6. **Designate "Phone-Free" Zones**: Establish certain areas in your home as "phone-free" zones, such as the dining table, living room, or bedroom. Creating these spaces encourages quality interactions and tech-free relaxation, reinforcing the habit of stepping away from screens.

How to Use Social Media Mindfully to Enhance Well-Being

Social media can be a powerful tool for staying connected, but it can also contribute to stress, comparison, and feelings of inadequacy, especially during the holidays. Practicing mindful social media use helps to reduce these negative impacts, enhancing our holiday well-being.

1. **Curate Your Feed for Positivity**: Follow accounts that inspire, uplift, or bring you joy rather than those that lead to comparison or stress. Curating a positive feed allows you to engage with content that aligns with your values and brings you peace during the holiday season.
2. **Practice "Pause Before You Post"**: Before sharing on social media, pause and consider your intention. Are you sharing to connect, inspire, or spread joy, or is there pressure to present a perfect image? Mindful sharing can make social media a more positive experience, both for yourself and for those who follow you.
3. **Limit Comparison**: Social media often highlights idealized versions of reality, making it easy to fall into the trap of comparison. Remind yourself that what you see online doesn't always reflect real life. If you find yourself feeling inadequate or envious, take a break and focus on gratitude for your unique experiences and blessings.
4. **Engage Meaningfully, Not Mindlessly**: Instead of mindlessly scrolling, use social media to engage meaningfully with others. Comment thoughtfully, reach out to friends, or share a positive message. Meaningful engagement helps to foster real connections, making social media a more fulfilling experience.
5. **Take Social Media Sabbaths**: Consider taking one day each week during the holidays as a "social media Sabbath," a day entirely free from social media. This practice provides a regular, refreshing break from the digital world, helping to restore balance and presence in your life.

Limiting screen time and practicing mindful social media use are powerful ways to enhance holiday well-being. By creating boundaries around technology, you create space for presence, joy, and genuine connection, making the holiday season more meaningful and fulfilling.

Creating Tech-Free Holiday Traditions

The holidays offer a perfect opportunity to craft traditions that prioritize face-to-face connection, creativity, and presence. Establishing tech-free traditions can strengthen bonds with loved ones, spark joy, and create memorable experiences that aren't diluted by digital distractions. Here, we'll explore ideas for creating tech-free holiday traditions that foster connection and enrich the holiday spirit.

Crafting Activities and Experiences That Prioritize Connection Over Screen Time

Engaging in tech-free activities brings the focus back to authentic interactions, creativity, and shared joy. Here are some ideas for holiday traditions that allow you to step away from screens and immerse yourself in meaningful experiences:

1. **Host a "No-Phones" Holiday Gathering**: Encourage friends and family to leave their phones in a designated area during gatherings, allowing everyone to fully engage in conversation and activities. This small adjustment creates an environment of presence and connection, making the time together feel richer and more meaningful.
2. **Cook or Bake Together**: Cooking and baking together is a hands-on, creative activity that encourages teamwork and conversation. Whether making holiday

cookies, traditional meals, or experimenting with new recipes, spending time in the kitchen allows you to connect without digital distractions. Enjoying the finished product together only adds to the joy.

3. **Play Board Games or Card Games**: Bring back the charm of classic games, such as board games or card games, as a way to bond with family and friends. Games encourage friendly competition, laughter, and collaboration, creating a warm, screen-free environment. Choose games that are inclusive, engaging, and lighthearted for all ages.

4. **Create Handwritten Holiday Cards or Letters**: Instead of digital greetings, write handwritten holiday cards or letters to friends and family. This thoughtful gesture feels more personal and meaningful, and the process of writing by hand allows for moments of reflection and appreciation. You might even involve loved ones by creating a card-making station with art supplies.

5. **Go on a Nature Walk or Hike**: Spend time outdoors with loved ones, enjoying a nature walk, hike, or simply exploring a nearby park. Being in nature fosters peace, gratitude, and connection to the world around you. As a bonus, it also allows everyone to recharge away from screens, surrounded by the beauty of the season.

6. **Host a DIY Craft Night**: Crafting is an enjoyable, screen-free activity that allows for creativity and bonding. Gather materials for a holiday craft night where everyone can create something meaningful, such as homemade ornaments, wreaths, or candles. Crafting together encourages conversation and

laughter, resulting in both memories and unique creations.
7. **Read Aloud or Share Stories**: Reading aloud, sharing family stories, or even taking turns telling holiday-themed tales creates a sense of closeness and nostalgia. Consider reading from a favorite book, sharing holiday memories, or making up stories as a family. This tradition fosters intimacy and allows everyone to engage with each other in a relaxed, meaningful way.
8. **Practice a Family Gratitude Ritual**: Start or end each gathering with a gratitude ritual where everyone shares something they're grateful for. This tradition emphasizes the importance of connection and appreciation, reinforcing the spirit of the season. The simple act of sharing gratitude promotes positivity and unity, enhancing the holiday experience.

Tech-Free Traditions for Personal Reflection and Connection

Unplugging for personal reflection during the holidays can create a sense of peace, grounding, and gratitude. These solo tech-free traditions allow you to reconnect with yourself and foster a deeper understanding of your own experiences:

1. **Journal Your Reflections and Goals**: Spend time journaling your reflections on the past year, noting lessons learned, meaningful experiences, and areas for growth. Setting goals or intentions for the coming year can create a sense of purpose and excitement, turning the holiday season into a time of personal renewal.

2. **Practice Mindful Meditation**: Take a few minutes each day for mindful meditation, focusing on your breath, gratitude, or a positive intention. Meditation encourages a calm mind and heart, helping to reduce stress and increase awareness during the holiday season.
3. **Create a Vision Board for the New Year**: Reflect on your goals, aspirations, and dreams, and create a vision board to represent them. Cut out images, words, or symbols from magazines, or draw your own pictures to create a tangible reminder of your goals. This tech-free tradition allows you to visualize the future you want to create, fostering a sense of optimism.
4. **Dedicate Time to Reading a Meaningful Book**: Choose a book that brings you joy, inspiration, or comfort, and set aside time to read it in a cozy, tech-free setting. Reading offers a quiet escape and a chance to explore new perspectives, allowing you to recharge and gain insights for the year ahead.
5. **Create a Gratitude Jar**: Start a gratitude jar where you write down things you're thankful for each day or week. Over time, the jar will fill with positive reflections, serving as a visual reminder of the season's blessings. Reviewing these notes at the end of the year can create a powerful sense of appreciation.

Unplugging from technology doesn't mean disconnecting from the joys of the season; rather, it allows us to immerse ourselves fully in the experiences and people who bring meaning to our lives. By creating tech-free traditions and practicing mindful screen use, we foster genuine connection, personal reflection, and a holiday experience that feels rejuvenating and true to our well-being.

The Stress-Free Holiday Wellness Guide: Mindful Self-Care and Int...

Unplugging and recharging during the holidays is about finding balance, using technology with intention, and creating traditions that prioritize connection and presence. By limiting screen time, practicing mindful social media use, and establishing tech-free activities, we create space to enjoy the holiday season in its fullest sense. This intentional approach to technology allows us to reconnect with what matters most, making the holiday experience richer, calmer, and more fulfilling.

As we approach the close of this guide, remember that the holidays offer an invitation to pause, reflect, and reconnect—with ourselves, our loved ones, and our goals for the coming year. Through mindful engagement, nurturing relationships, and intentional self-care, you can craft a holiday experience that not only honors your well-being but also sets a foundation for a balanced, fulfilling year ahead.

Chapter 9
Creating New, Wellness-Oriented Holiday Traditions

As we grow and evolve, so too can the ways we celebrate the holidays. Shifting our focus to wellness-oriented traditions allows us to celebrate the season with greater authenticity, balance, and purpose. By reimagining existing customs and integrating new ones centered on well-being, nature, creativity, and kindness, we can transform the holidays into a time that fosters health, connection, and personal growth. This chapter explores how to modernize old traditions to better align with current needs, as well as the role that acts of kindness play in creating meaningful connections and boosting mental well-being.

Reimagining Old Traditions

Holiday traditions can carry immense sentimental value, connecting us to loved ones and cherished memories. However, some traditions may no longer fit with our values, lifestyle, or current needs. Reimagining holiday traditions to incorporate wellness, creativity, and nature can offer a fresh sense of meaning, making the season more enjoyable and personally fulfilling. In this section, we'll explore ways to modernize holiday customs and create new traditions that honor well-being.

How to Modernize or Transform Holiday Traditions to Suit Your Current Needs

Transforming old traditions to suit your present self can make the holidays feel more authentic and aligned with your wellness goals. Here are some ideas for modernizing traditions:

1. **Redefine Gift-Giving**: Traditional gift-giving can sometimes feel materialistic or burdensome, especially if you feel pressure to buy numerous gifts. Consider redefining this tradition by giving experiences rather than objects, like tickets to a concert, a gift certificate for a favorite restaurant, or a membership to a museum. This shift emphasizes meaningful experiences over material items.
2. **Create a "Mindfulness Morning" Tradition**: Mornings during the holidays can be chaotic, especially if there are gatherings and preparations to manage. Establish a "mindfulness morning" tradition, where you begin each day with a short meditation, breathing exercise, or gratitude practice. This

grounding ritual can set a peaceful tone for the rest of the day.
3. **Celebrate a "Day of Rest and Reflection"**: Many holiday traditions involve constant activity, which can be exhausting. Consider setting aside one day during the season as a "day of rest and reflection." Use this day to relax, journal, meditate, or engage in quiet activities. This tradition offers a refreshing pause amid the holiday rush, allowing you to reconnect with yourself.
4. **Replace Alcoholic Toasts with Non-Alcoholic Alternatives**: If holiday gatherings typically involve alcoholic drinks, consider introducing non-alcoholic options, such as mocktails or infused water. Offering these alternatives supports those who may prefer not to drink and creates a more inclusive environment.
5. **Adopt Sustainable Decorating**: Decorating can feel wasteful when it involves disposable or single-use items. Reimagine this tradition by using sustainable materials, like natural elements (pinecones, greenery, dried citrus) or handmade decorations that can be reused each year. Decorating sustainably not only reduces waste but also aligns with values of environmental responsibility.

Ideas for New Traditions Centered Around Well-Being, Nature, and Creativity

Incorporating wellness, nature, and creativity into holiday traditions can bring a sense of joy, grounding, and fulfillment to the season. Here are ideas for new traditions that prioritize personal well-being:

1. **Nature Walk or Hike**: Start a tradition of going on a nature walk or hike with friends or family. Time spent in nature can be incredibly grounding and rejuvenating, helping you connect with both loved ones and the natural world. If you live near scenic areas, consider choosing a different trail each year to keep the tradition fresh.
2. **Crafting and Creative Nights**: Host a crafting night where you make homemade decorations, ornaments, or gifts. Gather art supplies, invite loved ones, and spend the evening creating. Engaging in creativity is relaxing and offers a rewarding, screen-free way to connect with others.
3. **Reflective Journaling and Goal-Setting**: Use the holiday season to start a tradition of reflective journaling and goal-setting. Spend time journaling about the past year's experiences, noting lessons learned, personal growth, and moments of joy. This tradition can help bring closure to the year and set positive intentions for the new one.
4. **Mindful Eating Celebrations**: If you usually have a holiday feast, consider incorporating mindful eating practices. Begin the meal by expressing gratitude, savoring each bite, and pausing between courses. This practice enhances the sensory enjoyment of the meal and encourages everyone to slow down, connect, and appreciate the food.
5. **Book Exchange and Quiet Reading**: Host a book exchange with friends or family, where each person brings a favorite book to gift. After the exchange, set aside time for quiet reading together, enjoying a cozy, shared moment of stillness. This

tradition is ideal for book lovers and those who enjoy calm, relaxing activities.
6. **Holiday Gratitude Circle**: Begin a tradition of gathering in a circle, where each person shares something they are grateful for. This simple practice can foster a sense of connection, unity, and positivity, creating a warm, supportive atmosphere. Practicing gratitude together can also help bring everyone into the present, reminding us of the blessings that the season brings.

Reimagining traditions to focus on well-being, nature, and creativity allows us to align the holiday season with our personal growth and health. These traditions honor the values of mindfulness, sustainability, and connection, offering an approach to the holidays that feels nurturing, intentional, and balanced.

Incorporating Acts of Kindness and Giving

Acts of kindness and generosity have long been part of the holiday season, but shifting focus from materialism to meaningful giving can create a deeper sense of fulfillment. Volunteering, donating, or simply practicing small acts of kindness can increase feelings of purpose, enhance mental well-being, and strengthen connections with others. This section explores how acts of kindness boost well-being and offers ideas for holiday traditions that emphasize compassion over materialism.

How Generosity and Volunteering Boost Mental Health

Giving to others, whether through time, resources, or kindness, is linked to numerous mental health benefits, including increased happiness, reduced stress, and a greater sense of purpose. Here's how generosity can positively impact well-being during the holidays:

1. **Enhances Sense of Purpose**: Helping others creates a sense of purpose, reminding us of our ability to make a positive impact. This feeling of purpose can reduce feelings of isolation and sadness, replacing them with gratitude and connection.
2. **Boosts Mood through "Helper's High"**: Acts of kindness release endorphins, often referred to as a "helper's high." This natural mood boost creates a sense of happiness and fulfillment, making giving a rewarding experience for both the giver and the recipient.
3. **Increases Social Connection**: Engaging in acts of generosity, especially when done with others, strengthens social bonds and fosters a sense of community. Whether volunteering, giving gifts, or practicing small acts of kindness, generosity promotes positive interactions and meaningful relationships.
4. **Reduces Stress and Anxiety**: Helping others can shift focus away from personal worries, providing perspective and reducing stress. The simple act of giving allows us to concentrate on others' needs, which can be grounding and comforting, especially amid holiday pressures.
5. **Encourages Gratitude**: Practicing generosity can foster gratitude, helping us appreciate what we have. This gratitude cultivates a mindset of abundance, reducing the pressure to focus on materialism and increasing satisfaction with simpler joys.

Shifting the Focus from Materialism to Meaningful Connection

Refocusing the holiday season on giving, kindness, and connection allows us to experience the holidays in a more meaningful way. Here are some ideas for creating traditions that emphasize compassion and connection over material gifts:

1. **Family Volunteering Day**: Start a tradition of volunteering together as a family, whether at a local shelter, food bank, or community organization. Volunteering as a group fosters a sense of shared purpose and community connection, helping everyone feel united in kindness.
2. **"Secret Santa" Acts of Kindness**: Instead of traditional gift exchanges, organize a "Secret Santa" where each person performs a random act of kindness for someone else. This could include anything from leaving an encouraging note to helping with a task. These small gestures of kindness create a festive atmosphere filled with positivity and gratitude.
3. **Donation Drive in Lieu of Gifts**: Consider organizing a family donation drive where each person contributes items for a cause or charity. Choose a cause that resonates with your family, such as donating winter clothing to a homeless shelter, toys for children, or food for local pantries. The act of giving can feel more fulfilling than traditional gifts.
4. **Storytelling and Sharing Memories**: Dedicate time during holiday gatherings for storytelling and memory-sharing. Encourage family members to share their favorite holiday memories or stories of kindness they've experienced. This tradition fosters a sense of

connection, focusing on the power of shared history and love over material gifts.

5. **Holiday Letter Writing for Neighbors or Friends**: Instead of buying gifts, write letters to friends, neighbors, or family members. Expressing appreciation and gratitude through a heartfelt letter creates a memorable keepsake and shifts the focus from physical gifts to words of kindness and thoughtfulness.
6. **Create a "Kindness Advent Calendar"**: Instead of a traditional advent calendar with treats or gifts, create a kindness calendar. Each day of the holiday season, choose a small act of kindness to complete, such as complimenting someone, donating to a cause, or making someone smile. This tradition emphasizes daily acts of compassion, creating a positive ripple effect in your community.
7. **Host a "Giving Gathering"**: If you're hosting a holiday gathering, ask guests to bring items to donate rather than personal gifts. Select a charity together and make it a group goal to collect items, such as canned goods, warm clothing, or toys for a children's hospital. This tradition brings a collective spirit of giving to your gathering.

Incorporating acts of kindness and emphasizing meaningful connection over materialism reshapes the holiday season into a celebration of compassion, unity, and joy. These traditions encourage everyone to engage in the season with open hearts, enhancing mental well-being and deepening the connections between loved ones and the community.

Reimagining holiday traditions with a focus on wellness, nature, and kindness allows us to create a season that is more reflective, balanced, and fulfilling. By transforming old customs, adopting practices that support well-being, and shifting our attention from materialism to meaningful connection, the holidays become a time of personal growth, compassion, and authentic joy. These wellness-oriented traditions remind us that the spirit of the season is not found in possessions but in the love we give, the gratitude we cultivate, and the kindness we share.

As you consider your holiday traditions, allow yourself the freedom to create practices that resonate with who you are today. Whether spending time in nature, crafting creative projects, or volunteering as a family, these traditions foster a deeper sense of connection, gratitude, and wellness. Embrace this season as an opportunity to renew your sense of purpose and joy, creating holiday memories that truly enrich your heart and spirit.

Chapter 10
Reflecting and Preparing for the New Year with a Wellness Focus

The close of the holiday season and the start of a new year offer an ideal moment for reflection and renewal. Rather than the pressure of typical New Year's resolutions, a wellness-oriented approach prioritizes intentions that support mental, emotional, and physical well-being. Taking time to reflect on the past year, honor your growth, and set meaningful intentions for the future allows you to step into the new year with clarity, self-compassion, and a sense of purpose. This chapter explores practices for reflecting on the past year with gratitude and compassion, as well as methods for crafting intentions and goals that foster balance and wellness throughout the year.

The Power of Reflection

Reflection allows us to pause, recognize our growth, and gain insights from our experiences. This practice can bring closure to the past year and foster a sense of gratitude and self-acceptance. Reflecting with a wellness focus involves acknowledging both triumphs and challenges, seeing them as integral parts of our personal journey. In this section, we explore practices that support reflective insight, encouraging gratitude, compassion, and mental wellness as we look back on the year.

Practices for Reflecting on the Past Year with Gratitude and Compassion

Reflection can be a powerful tool for personal growth, as it enables us to acknowledge our progress, make peace with challenges, and approach the new year with a fresh perspective. Here are practices for reflecting on the past year with a spirit of gratitude and compassion:

1. **Gratitude Journaling**: Take time to reflect on the people, experiences, and moments you're grateful for from the past year. Consider starting a gratitude journal entry where you list these highlights, noting why each was meaningful. Reflecting on moments of joy, connection, or achievement can cultivate a sense of gratitude that energizes you for the year ahead.
2. **Create a "Year in Review" Mind Map**: A mind map allows you to visually explore your experiences from the past year. Start by placing "2023" in the center, then add branches for key areas

like relationships, health, career, and personal growth. Reflect on each branch, noting events or milestones. This activity can help you see your journey at a glance, revealing patterns, insights, and growth.
3. **Practice Self-Compassion Reflection**: Reflection is most effective when approached with self-compassion. Rather than focusing on perceived failures, acknowledge the efforts you made and the challenges you overcame. Reflect on areas where you felt vulnerable, and give yourself credit for navigating them. Self-compassion can transform regret into learning, helping you carry wisdom into the new year.
4. **List Lessons Learned**: Consider creating a list of lessons you've learned throughout the year. These could be insights into personal resilience, understanding about relationships, or even practical skills you've acquired. This practice brings awareness to the knowledge you've gained, reinforcing your ability to grow and adapt.
5. **Celebrate Personal Milestones and Achievements**: Reflect on moments of growth or accomplishments, both big and small. Celebrating personal milestones, whether they're related to work, relationships, or self-care, allows you to appreciate your progress. This focus on success boosts confidence and encourages you to build on these achievements in the year ahead.

Setting Intentions for Mental and Emotional Wellness in the Year Ahead

Once you've reflected on the past year, setting wellness-oriented intentions can help guide you toward a balanced and fulfilling future. Rather than setting rigid goals, these intentions focus on how you want to feel, grow, and take care of yourself mentally and emotionally.

1. **Identify Core Values and Priorities**: Begin by identifying the core values that matter most to you, such as compassion, creativity, connection, or resilience. Use these values as a foundation for your intentions, aligning your goals with what truly resonates with you.
2. **Set Wellness Intentions**: Think about specific areas of wellness you'd like to prioritize, such as mental clarity, emotional balance, physical health, or spiritual growth. Craft intentions that support these areas, such as "I will practice self-care daily" or "I will prioritize my mental well-being by taking regular breaks and setting boundaries."
3. **Choose an Anchor Word**: An anchor word, like "peace," "growth," "balance," or "joy," can serve as a guiding principle throughout the year. Choose a word that reflects the essence of your wellness focus. Whenever you need clarity, return to this word as a reminder of your intentions.
4. **Create Affirmations for Wellness**: Positive affirmations help reinforce intentions, turning them into daily reminders for self-care and compassion. Create affirmations that encourage mental and emotional wellness, such as "I am worthy of rest," "I am open to growth and change," or "I am at peace with where I am." Reciting these affirmations can help keep you aligned with your intentions.
5. **Visualize Your Ideal Year**: Spend a few moments visualizing what a balanced, fulfilling year might look like for you. Imagine yourself embodying your

wellness intentions, setting boundaries, practicing self-care, and prioritizing mental health. Visualization can bring clarity and motivation, helping you see the potential for positive change in the new year.

Reflecting on the past year with gratitude and compassion, while setting intentions that prioritize well-being, enables you to enter the new year with a sense of clarity, confidence, and purpose. These practices encourage self-acceptance, inner peace, and a renewed commitment to wellness.

Creating a Wellness-Oriented New Year's Ritual

Starting the year with a wellness-focused ritual can help reinforce your commitment to self-care and mental health. Rather than traditional resolutions focused solely on achievements, wellness-oriented rituals emphasize balance, self-compassion, and personal growth. This section provides guidance for crafting resolutions and intentions that support mental and emotional health, as well as simple goal-setting techniques that promote sustainable wellness throughout the year.

Crafting Resolutions or Intentions that Prioritize Self-Care and Mental Health

Resolutions that prioritize well-being focus on how we want to experience life and care for ourselves rather than on specific outcomes. These intentions are flexible, allowing for growth and adaptability while supporting self-compassion and balance. Here are ways to create resolutions that emphasize self-care and mental health:

1. **Set Gentle, Attainable Goals**: Rather than setting highly ambitious goals, choose intentions that feel achievable and nurturing. For example, instead of

"Exercise every day," try "Move my body regularly in ways that feel good to me." This approach allows for flexibility and accommodates changes in motivation or energy.

2. **Focus on Habits Over Results**: Center your resolutions on habits that contribute to your well-being. Instead of focusing on an end result, like "lose weight" or "earn a promotion," shift your focus to positive habits like "make time for physical activity" or "engage in creative work." This mindset emphasizes consistent effort over outcomes, which can reduce stress and encourage steady progress.

3. **Incorporate Emotional Wellness Practices**: Include practices specifically aimed at emotional health, such as "I will journal my feelings each week" or "I will schedule one activity each month that brings me joy." Emotional wellness resolutions nurture your mental well-being and help you stay connected to what brings you peace and happiness.

4. **Commit to a Self-Care Ritual**: Establishing a regular self-care ritual, such as a weekly "me-time" hour or a monthly day for relaxation, supports mental health and prevents burnout. Make this ritual a non-negotiable part of your routine to ensure that self-care remains a priority throughout the year.

5. **Practice Forgiveness for Slip-Ups**: Change can be challenging, and setbacks are a natural part of growth. Include a resolution to forgive yourself when things don't go as planned. Self-forgiveness is crucial in creating a wellness-oriented mindset that prioritizes resilience over perfection.

Simple Goal-Setting Techniques for Maintaining Balance and Well-Being

Effective goal-setting techniques ensure that wellness intentions are sustainable, adaptable, and supportive of long-term balance. Here are some methods to help you maintain well-being while pursuing personal growth:

1. **Use the SMART Goal Framework**: SMART goals—specific, measurable, achievable, relevant, and time-bound—can make your intentions clearer and more manageable. For example, instead of "Be more active," a SMART goal would be "Take a 30-minute walk three times a week." Setting SMART goals helps break down your wellness intentions into actionable steps.
2. **Set Quarterly Check-Ins**: Checking in with your intentions every three months can help you stay on track without feeling overwhelmed. During these check-ins, review your goals, celebrate progress, and adjust as needed. Quarterly reviews encourage reflection and allow for flexibility, supporting a balanced approach to your goals.
3. **Practice the "Three Wins" Method**: Each week, write down three small "wins" related to your wellness intentions. These could include small victories, like "I took a walk when I was feeling stressed" or "I completed my morning meditation." Celebrating wins, however small, reinforces positive habits and builds momentum.
4. **Break Down Goals into "Micro-Goals"**: Large goals can feel daunting, making it easy to lose motivation. Breaking down goals into smaller, manageable "micro-goals" allows you to progress

gradually. For instance, if your goal is to practice mindfulness, start by setting a micro-goal of five minutes of mindfulness each day, gradually increasing as you build the habit.

5. **Create a "Self-Care Accountability Buddy"**: Partner with a friend or family member who also has wellness intentions. Check in with each other weekly or monthly to celebrate achievements, discuss challenges, and encourage one another. Accountability can be a motivating factor, and sharing the journey with someone else adds a sense of support and encouragement.

6. **End Each Month with Reflection**: At the end of each month, take a few moments to reflect on your progress. Review what worked well, what you enjoyed, and any areas for adjustment. Monthly reflection ensures that you're staying aligned with your intentions and encourages adaptability, making your wellness journey more sustainable.

Creating a wellness-oriented New Year's ritual prioritizes self-care, mental health, and emotional well-being. By setting compassionate resolutions and using flexible, supportive goal-setting techniques, you foster a balanced approach to personal growth that honors your needs and aspirations.

Reflecting on the past year and setting intentions for the next with a wellness focus allows us to approach the new year with mindfulness, gratitude, and self-compassion. By looking back on the lessons and joys of the past year, we gain insights that shape our path forward. Setting wellness-oriented goals and engaging in rituals that prioritize mental, emotional, and physical health ensure that our resolutions remain sustainable, adaptable, and fulfilling.

As you enter this new chapter, embrace the opportunity to cultivate habits, intentions, and self-care practices that support a balanced and nourishing year. With thoughtful reflection and purpose-driven goals, you set the stage for a year of growth, resilience, and genuine well-being, creating a foundation for lasting happiness and peace

Afterword

As we bring this journey to a close, it's essential to recognize that the wellness-focused practices, reflections, and traditions explored throughout this book are not solely for the holiday season. These approaches are foundational tools that, when woven into our everyday lives, have the potential to sustain well-being, enhance resilience, and bring balance to our entire year. From setting compassionate boundaries and prioritizing mental health to engaging in meaningful relationships and honoring our own needs,

Afterword

the journey to wellness is continuous and rewarding. In this final chapter, we explore ways to sustain these practices beyond the holidays, integrating them into daily routines for long-term balance and fulfillment.

Sustaining Wellness Beyond the Holidays

The energy and introspection of the holiday season provide a fertile ground for cultivating wellness-oriented habits. However, as the season fades, there can be a tendency to fall back into familiar patterns of overcommitment, stress, and distraction. Sustaining wellness beyond the holidays involves integrating the self-care, mindfulness, and intentionality practiced during the season into everyday life, helping you approach each day with a renewed sense of balance, purpose, and joy. Here, we discuss ways to carry these wellness practices forward and make them part of your ongoing routine.

Integrating Wellness Practices into Everyday Life Post-Holiday Season

Taking the wellness rituals and routines established during the holidays and adapting them for everyday life allows for greater continuity and consistency. Here are ways to seamlessly incorporate these practices year-round:

1. **Daily Morning and Evening Rituals**: Begin and end each day with small wellness rituals that ground and center you. Mornings could include a brief mindfulness practice, a few minutes of journaling, or simply setting an intention for the day. Evenings can be a time for gratitude reflection, calming breaths, or winding down with a book. These rituals foster a sense of balance and presence, helping you maintain the grounding energy from the holidays.

Afterword

2. **Regular Check-Ins for Reflection and Intention-Setting**: Just as you reflected on the past year during the holidays, making regular check-ins part of your routine supports ongoing growth and self-awareness. Weekly or monthly check-ins can help you stay aligned with your intentions, assess your well-being, and adjust your habits as needed. This reflection doesn't have to be time-consuming—a few minutes spent in thoughtful review can bring significant clarity and focus.
3. **Mindful Eating as a Daily Practice**: Mindful eating, practiced during holiday meals, is a powerful tool for appreciating food and improving digestion. Continue this practice by slowing down at mealtimes, savoring each bite, and engaging all your senses. This simple habit not only supports physical health but also brings awareness to your relationship with food, enhancing well-being.
4. **Celebrating Small Moments of Joy**: The holiday season often highlights moments of joy and gratitude. Extend this by creating a habit of celebrating small, everyday moments—such as a walk in nature, a shared laugh, or a quiet cup of tea. Finding joy in these simple pleasures can enhance your overall happiness and remind you of the beauty in daily life.
5. **Prioritizing Rest and Reflection Days**: The "day of rest" concept practiced during the holidays can serve as a rejuvenating habit throughout the year. Designate one day each month or quarter as a "wellness day" for rest, reflection, and activities that nurture your well-being. These days can help prevent burnout, promote balance, and keep you attuned to your mental and emotional needs.

6. **Maintaining Seasonal and Nature-Inspired Rituals**: The connection to nature established during the holidays can continue year-round. Mark each season's arrival by spending time outdoors, noting seasonal changes, or bringing natural elements into your home. These nature-inspired rituals keep you connected to the world around you, grounding you and promoting a sense of calm.

Maintaining Boundaries, Self-Care, and Mindfulness Throughout the Year

The healthy boundaries, self-care routines, and mindful practices cultivated during the holidays can help structure a more balanced and fulfilling lifestyle. Maintaining these habits beyond the season fosters resilience and reduces stress, allowing you to engage with the world from a place of strength and peace.

1. **Upholding Personal Boundaries**: During the holidays, you may have practiced saying "no" to excessive obligations or setting limits on social events. Upholding these boundaries throughout the year allows you to protect your time and energy, preventing overwhelm. This may mean setting boundaries around work hours, social commitments, or even screen time to ensure a balanced lifestyle.
2. **Continuing Self-Care Routines**: Make self-care a regular, non-negotiable part of your routine. Whether through weekly self-care nights, monthly spa days, or daily moments of mindfulness, self-care allows you to recharge and reconnect with yourself. Regular self-care rituals support your mental and physical health, helping you sustain a sense of well-being and balance throughout the year.

Afterword

3. **Incorporating Mindfulness into Daily Life**: Practicing mindfulness beyond the holidays can enhance focus, reduce stress, and increase appreciation for the present moment. Take short mindfulness breaks during the day—whether through deep breathing, a mindful walk, or a moment of stillness—to bring awareness and peace into your daily routine.
4. **Checking in on Social Media and Technology Boundaries**: The digital detox practiced during the holidays can continue with intentional use of technology year-round. Set limits on screen time, designate tech-free zones, or practice social media "fasts" to reduce dependency. Conscious tech use helps preserve mental clarity, improve focus, and foster meaningful offline connections.
5. **Balancing Goals with Self-Compassion**: While goal-setting can be motivating, maintaining a mindset of self-compassion is key to long-term growth. Approach your goals with flexibility, understanding that setbacks are part of the process. Balancing ambition with self-compassion allows for sustainable progress, helping you achieve your intentions while honoring your mental and emotional well-being.

By integrating wellness practices into everyday life, you can sustain the sense of purpose, peace, and joy cultivated during the holidays. These practices serve as anchors, bringing stability and clarity amid life's demands and allowing you to navigate each day with resilience and intention.

Afterword

Embracing a Year-Round Wellness Journey

As you move forward, carrying these wellness principles into the new year offers a path toward personal fulfillment and resilience. Each practice, ritual, and reflection explored in this book is a building block for a balanced, meaningful life—a life where your well-being remains at the forefront. Embracing wellness as an ongoing journey rather than a destination allows you to evolve, adapt, and deepen your connection with yourself and others.

Cultivating Wellness as a Lifelong Practice

The practices you've developed during the holidays can become lifelong habits, creating a continuous cycle of renewal, growth, and self-discovery. Here's how to sustain wellness as a year-round journey:

1. **Approach Life with Curiosity and Openness**: Wellness is dynamic, evolving as you grow. Embrace curiosity, experimenting with new self-care practices, wellness rituals, and ways of connecting with others. This openness keeps your journey fresh, adaptable, and suited to your changing needs.
2. **Create Wellness Goals with a Flexible Approach**: Use goal-setting techniques that support well-being, allowing room for adjustments along the way. Set intentions that align with your values, prioritize self-compassion, and adapt as necessary. Remember, wellness is a journey, and flexibility allows you to navigate it with grace.
3. **Establish Regular Reflection Periods**: Regularly reflecting on your journey helps you stay connected to your intentions and goals. Set aside time every quarter or season to review your wellness practices, celebrate progress, and set new intentions.

Afterword

These reflection periods encourage mindful growth, supporting balance and alignment.

4. **Embrace Community and Connection**: Wellness is not a solitary journey; building connections with others who value well-being can deepen your experience. Seek out supportive communities, wellness groups, or friends who share similar goals, encouraging each other and celebrating shared growth.
5. **Nurture Your Mind, Body, and Spirit Equally**: Wellness encompasses more than one aspect of life; it is a holistic approach that involves nurturing the mind, body, and spirit. Maintain practices that address each area, such as mental health check-ins, physical activity, and time for spiritual or reflective pursuits. This balanced approach promotes harmony, helping you thrive in all areas of life.
6. **Revisit and Reinvent Traditions as Needed**: Over time, your needs, values, and priorities may shift. Revisit your wellness practices and traditions each year, refining or reinventing them to stay relevant and meaningful. These intentional changes allow your wellness journey to stay aligned with who you are becoming.

Maintaining a Positive and Grateful Mindset

A positive, grateful mindset enhances resilience, brings fulfillment to daily life, and creates a foundation of joy. Practicing gratitude regularly, seeking joy in small moments, and acknowledging growth can help you maintain a balanced, grounded outlook.

1. **Practice Daily Gratitude**: Make gratitude a daily habit by noting something you're thankful for each

Afterword

day, whether in a journal or during moments of quiet reflection. This practice shifts focus to the positive, creating a foundation of abundance and contentment.

2. **Celebrate Small Wins and Milestones**: Acknowledge and celebrate your progress along the wellness journey, no matter how small. Every positive choice, act of self-care, or moment of clarity is a step forward. Celebrating small wins builds confidence, motivating you to continue prioritizing well-being.
3. **Seek Joy in Simple Moments**: Wellness isn't about grand gestures; it's about cultivating joy in everyday moments. Whether it's savoring a morning coffee, appreciating a sunset, or laughing with a friend, small moments of joy infuse life with meaning and connection.
4. **Stay Mindful of Your Inner Dialogue**: A positive mindset is supported by a compassionate inner dialogue. Be gentle with yourself, practicing kindness in thoughts and words. This approach reduces stress, fosters resilience, and encourages self-acceptance.
5. **Reflect on Personal Growth and Progress**: At various points in the year, reflect on how far you've come. Acknowledge the changes, growth, and insights gained along the way. Reflecting on personal progress encourages self-compassion and gratitude for the journey, reinforcing your commitment to wellness.

By nurturing a positive and grateful mindset, you build a solid foundation for sustaining well-being, resilience, and joy in the year ahead. This outlook enhances your wellness journey, transforming each day into an opportunity for connection, balance, and growth.

Afterword

Final Reflections

The wellness-focused practices explored in this book offer a path to a balanced, fulfilling life. By embracing reflection, cultivating meaningful connections, and setting intentional goals, you've laid the groundwork for a year of well-being, joy, and resilience. These practices are more than holiday traditions—they are tools to sustain a healthy, mindful life that supports your evolving journey.

As you carry these principles into the year ahead, remember that wellness is a continuous process. By prioritizing self-care, mindfulness, and meaningful connection, you create a life that honors your unique needs and aspirations. Embrace the journey with an open heart, trusting that each step brings you closer to a life of balance, growth, and lasting fulfillment.

Appendices: Wellness Recourses

To support your wellness journey beyond the holidays, this appendix provides a selection of recommended books, apps, and tools for mental health, mindfulness, self-care, and emotional well-being. Each resource is designed to complement the practices outlined in this guide, empowering you to continue cultivating balance, resilience, and self-compassion throughout the year.

Appendices: Wellness Recourses

Recommended Books

1. **The Gifts of Imperfection** by Brené Brown - *This inspiring book explores how embracing our imperfections can lead to a more authentic, wholehearted life. It encourages readers to cultivate self-compassion, courage, and a sense of worthiness.*
2. **Atomic Habits** by James Clear - *Clear provides actionable insights into building positive habits and breaking negative ones, making it easier to sustain wellness practices over time. This guide offers practical strategies to implement small changes that lead to lasting transformation.*
3. **Wherever You Go, There You Are** by Jon Kabat-Zinn - *A foundational text on mindfulness, this book introduces the reader to mindfulness practices that cultivate awareness, presence, and calm. Kabat-Zinn's accessible approach is ideal for those seeking to develop a regular meditation practice.*
4. **Radical Acceptance** by Tara Brach - *Through guided exercises and compassionate insights, Brach helps readers learn self-acceptance and manage difficult emotions. This book is a valuable resource for anyone looking to deepen their emotional well-being.*
5. **The Power of Now** by Eckhart Tolle - *A classic on mindfulness and presence, Tolle's book emphasizes the importance of living fully in the present moment to experience peace and joy. It's a valuable read for those looking to reduce anxiety and increase mental clarity.*
6. **Self-Compassion: The Proven Power of Being Kind to Yourself** by Kristin Neff - *\explore the transformative power of self-compassion and*

Appendices: Wellness Recourses

provides tools to practice kindness toward oneself, especially in times of stress or failure.

7. **The Joy of Less** by Francine Jay - *For those interested in simplifying their lives, this book offers insights on decluttering and embracing minimalism, helping readers focus on what truly brings joy and meaning.*

Appendices: Wellness Recourses

Recommended Apps

1. **Headspace** A widely-used app for meditation and mindfulness, Headspace offers guided sessions for various aspects of wellness, including stress reduction, focus, sleep, and self-care. Suitable for beginners and experienced meditators alike.
2. **Calm** With features like sleep stories, breathing exercises, and mindfulness meditations, Calm supports mental clarity, relaxation, and quality sleep. It also includes tools for managing anxiety and improving focus.
3. **Insight Timer** Insight Timer is a free meditation app with thousands of guided meditations and customizable timers. It includes resources for managing stress, cultivating gratitude, and improving sleep.
4. **Moodfit** Moodfit offers tools to track mood, establish goals, and practice gratitude. It's ideal for those interested in understanding their emotional patterns and working toward improved mental health.
5. **MyLife Meditation** This app personalizes meditation and wellness suggestions based on how you're feeling. It includes short, guided meditations and relaxation exercises tailored to your emotional state.
6. **Fabulous** Fabulous focuses on building healthy routines through science-backed behavioral changes. It's an excellent app for those wanting to establish morning routines, exercise habits, and self-care practices.
7. **Shine** Shine is a self-care app offering daily inspiration, meditation, and mental health support. It is

Appendices: Wellness Recourses

designed to foster a positive mindset, encourage resilience, and reduce stress.

Appendices: Wellness Recourses

Recommended Tools

1. **Gratitude Journal -** *A simple gratitude journal can help you regularly reflect on things you're thankful for, promoting positivity and mental resilience. Many gratitude journals come with prompts to guide your reflections.*
2. **Bullet Journal** - *Bullet journals combine goal-setting, habit tracking, and creative planning in one customizable notebook. They're perfect for those who enjoy organizing wellness practices and tracking personal growth.*
3. **Yoga Mat** - *For those who practice yoga, mindfulness, or any movement-based self-care routine, a quality yoga mat is essential. Brands like Manduka and Gaiam offer mats that are durable, comfortable, and eco-friendly.*
4. **Essential Oil Diffuser** - *Aromatherapy can support relaxation, improve focus, and reduce stress. An essential oil diffuser allows you to enjoy the benefits of oils like lavender, eucalyptus, and peppermint, enhancing your environment and wellness practices.*
5. **Weighted Blanket** - *Weighted blankets are known for their calming effects, especially beneficial for those with anxiety or sleep disturbances. The added weight can help the body relax, improving sleep quality and reducing stress.*
6. **Habit Tracker** - *Physical or digital habit trackers help monitor daily wellness practices, from drinking water to practicing gratitude. Tracking progress visually can be motivating and encourage consistency.*
7. **Blue Light Blocking Glasses** - *For those spending time on screens, blue light blocking glasses*

Appendices: Wellness Recourses

reduce eye strain and promote better sleep. This tool is particularly useful if you're looking to reduce the impact of screen time on mental and physical health.

These resources are intended to support your wellness journey, providing tools to cultivate mindfulness, manage stress, and foster a balanced lifestyle. As you integrate these books, apps, and tools into your life, remember that wellness is a gradual journey. Consistency and self-compassion are key to making sustainable changes. May these resources empower you to continue nurturing your well-being, embracing each day with clarity, gratitude, and resilience.

Self-Care Checklist for the Holidays

This simple self-care checklist is designed to help you prioritize your well-being and maintain balance throughout the holiday season. Each item on the list reflects key strategies from this book, making it easy to incorporate wellness practices into even the busiest days. Refer to this checklist to stay grounded, centered, and aligned with your wellness goals.

Holiday Self-Care Checklist

1. Mindfulness and Presence

- ☐ **Start each day with a few minutes of mindfulness** (breathing exercises, morning meditation, or simply sitting in stillness).
- ☐ **Practice mindful eating** during holiday meals: savor each bite, pause between bites, and engage your senses.
- ☐ **Pause to appreciate small moments of joy** throughout the day (a quiet cup of tea, festive lights, laughter with loved ones).

2. Setting Boundaries and Protecting Energy

- ☐ **Say "no" to invitations or obligations that feel overwhelming** and focus on gatherings that bring genuine connection.
- ☐ **Limit screen time** and create tech-free times or spaces to fully engage with loved ones and reduce distractions.
- ☐ **Communicate your boundaries clearly**

with family and friends, especially around personal space, topics, or time commitments.

3. Physical Wellness and Movement

- ☐ **Incorporate gentle movement daily** (a walk outside, stretching, yoga, or even dancing to holiday music).
- ☐ **Prioritize restful sleep** by setting a consistent bedtime, avoiding screens before bed, and creating a calming nighttime routine.
- ☐ **Stay hydrated and limit caffeine and alcohol**, especially at social events, to keep energy levels balanced.

4. Emotional Health and Self-Compassion

- ☐ **Practice self-compassion in moments of stress**: recognize your emotions, validate them, and treat yourself kindly.
- ☐ **Let go of perfectionism** around holiday activities, decorations, and gatherings, and embrace the beauty in imperfections.
- ☐ **Forgive yourself for slip-ups or unmet expectations** and refocus on enjoying the present moment.

5. Reflection and Gratitude

- ☐ **Set aside time for gratitude reflection**, listing things you're thankful for each day to foster positivity.

Appendices: Wellness Recourses

- ☐ **Reflect on personal milestones or moments of joy** from the past year, celebrating your growth and accomplishments.
- ☐ **Create an anchor word or intention for the season**, such as "peace," "connection," or "gratitude," to remind yourself of your focus.

6. Simple Self-Care Practices

- ☐ **Take time for a weekly self-care ritual** (an at-home spa night, journaling session, or favorite creative activity).
- ☐ **Prepare nutritious, comforting meals** to nourish your body amid the abundance of holiday treats.
- ☐ **Incorporate moments of solitude when needed** to recharge, whether it's a walk, a quiet morning, or a few minutes of deep breathing.

7. Social Connections and Meaningful Interactions

- ☐ **Engage in quality conversations** and listen actively during gatherings to deepen connections.
- ☐ **Limit comparison with others**, especially on social media, and focus on your unique experience of the holidays.
- ☐ **Create or participate in acts of kindness** or giving, such as volunteering, donating, or supporting loved ones.

8. Embracing Nature and Seasonal Rituals

Appendices: Wellness Recourses

- ☐ **Spend time in nature** whenever possible, whether on a walk, hike, or simply enjoying fresh air.
- ☐ **Incorporate seasonal elements into your environment**, like natural decorations, candles, or cozy blankets.
- ☐ **Celebrate the winter season** by marking each solstice or change in weather, reflecting on the natural cycles around you.

Use this checklist as a quick reference throughout the holiday season. Remember that wellness is a journey, and even small acts of self-care can have a significant impact. Prioritizing your well-being allows you to navigate the holidays with resilience, presence, and joy, ensuring you feel nourished and balanced well into the new year.

Gratitude and Reflection Prompts

The holiday season is a wonderful time to pause, reflect, and focus on gratitude. These guided prompts can serve as a journal tool to help you connect with meaningful experiences, appreciate life's simple joys, and reflect on personal growth. Use these prompts during the holidays—or anytime you want to foster a deeper sense of peace, gratitude, and self-awareness.

Gratitude and Reflection Prompts for the Holidays
1. Seasonal Gratitude

- *What are three things about the winter season (or current season) that you're grateful for?*
- *What traditions or activities bring you joy during the holidays? How can you bring more of these into your life?*
- *Who has supported or inspired you this year? Reflect on what their support means to you.*

2. Reflecting on Personal Growth

- *What is one challenge you overcame this year? What did you learn from that experience?*
- *Reflect on a goal or intention you set earlier in the year. How has working toward it shaped you?*
- *How have your self-care or wellness practices evolved over the past year? What are you proud of?*

3. Celebrating Small Joys

- *What small, everyday moments have brought you the most happiness recently?*

- List five things that make you smile or bring you a sense of comfort during the holidays.
- Reflect on a recent experience that felt truly peaceful. What about that moment brought you calm?

4. Cultivating Connection

- Who are the people you're most grateful for right now? Why do they mean so much to you?
- What meaningful conversations or connections have you experienced recently? How did they impact you?
- Describe one way you'd like to show appreciation to a loved one during the holidays.

5. Honoring Loved Ones and Memories

- Is there a holiday memory with a loved one that brings you joy? Reflect on what made it special.
- Who are you thinking of this season, and how can you honor their memory or presence in your life?
- What is a family tradition or activity that you're grateful to be a part of? Why is it meaningful to you?

6. Looking Back with Gratitude

- What were the three most fulfilling experiences for you this past year?
- What lessons have you learned this year that you're grateful for? How will these lessons guide you in the future?
- Reflect on a positive change you made in your life this year. What inspired you to make it?

7. Setting Intentions for the New Year

- *What qualities or values do you want to focus on in the coming year?*
- *How would you like to grow in the year ahead? What small steps can you take to support this growth?*
- *What intentions or wellness goals feel most meaningful to you for the new year?*

8. Gratitude for Self-Compassion and Resilience

- *Write a message of gratitude to yourself for a difficult moment you navigated with strength.*
- *How have you practiced self-compassion this year? What can you do to continue this in the new year?*
- *What are three things you appreciate about who you are right now?*

9. Embracing Nature and Mindfulness

- *Reflect on a time you felt connected to nature this year. What about that moment was meaningful?*
- *How can you incorporate more time outdoors or in nature during the holiday season?*
- *List three sensory experiences you're grateful for (a scent, a sound, a taste, etc.). What do they bring to your life?*

10. Finding Peace in the Present Moment

- *What does "peace" mean to you this holiday season? How can you invite more of it into your days?*

Appendices: Wellness Recourses

- *Reflect on one thing you can let go of to create space for more calm and joy this season.*
- *Describe a moment when you felt truly present recently. What can you do to create more of these moments?*

These prompts are here to guide you in fostering gratitude and mindfulness, helping you stay grounded and connected to what matters most. Whether you use them daily, weekly, or simply as needed, let these questions serve as a gentle reminder to embrace self-compassion, celebrate growth, and honor the beauty of the present moment. May your reflections bring a sense of peace, clarity, and fulfillment to your holiday season and beyond.

More About Emma Grace Williams

Emma Grace Williams is a wellness coach, mindfulness teacher, and author specializing in practical approaches to mental health and balanced living. With a background in wellness coaching and over a decade of experience guiding clients through personal growth and self-care, Emma's mission is to make mindfulness and self-care accessible, meaningful, and transformative. She combines her knowledge of psychology, holistic wellness, and mindfulness practices to create tools and resources that empower others to build resilient, joyful lives.

Emma's journey into wellness writing began through her own experience navigating the pressures of the holiday season while balancing a busy life. Witnessing the challenges that many of her clients faced during high-stress times like the holidays, she saw a need for a guide that could help individuals maintain their well-being not only seasonally but all year round. Her latest book, *Mindful Holidays: A Guide to Seasonal Wellness and Year-Round Balance*, reflects her passion for helping people create sustainable wellness practices that bring peace, purpose, and joy.

When she's not writing or working with clients, Emma enjoys practicing yoga, gardening, and creating seasonal traditions with her family. She finds renewal in nature, and her love for simple, seasonal living is woven throughout her work, inspiring readers to find peace and joy in small, intentional moments. Emma believes that self-care is both a privilege and a responsibility and hopes her work inspires others to embrace wellness as a lifelong journey.

www.ingramcontent.com/pod-product-compliance
Lightning Source LLC
LaVergne TN
LVHW050024080526
838202LV00069B/6905